Knit Red

sixth&springbooks
NEW YORK

Knit Red

STITCHING FOR WOMEN'S HEART HEALTH

LAURA ZANDER

DEBORAH NORVILLE

♥ DEDICATION

To my husband, Doug. Everything that is good in my life (including this book!) is because of you.

sixth&springbooks

161 Avenue of the Americas, New York, NY 10013
sixthandspringbooks.com

Editorial Director
JOY AQUILINO

Senior Editor
MICHELLE BREDESON

Art Director
DIANE LAMPHRON

Yarn Editor
RENEE LORION

Associate Editor
ALEXANDRA JOINNIDES

Instructions Editors
PAT HARSTE
AMY POLCYN

Instructions Proofreader
CHARLOTTE PARRY

Copy Editor
LISA SILVERMAN

Technical Illustrations
ULI MONCH

Model Photography
ROSE CALLAHAN

Still-Life Photography
MARCUS TULLIS

Stylist & Bookings Manager
SARAH LIEBOWITZ

Hair & Makeup
ELENA LYAKIR

....

Vice President, Publisher
TRISHA MALCOLM

Creative Director
JOE VIOR

Production Manager
DAVID JOINNIDES

President
ART JOINNIDES

48657430
7/12

ISBN: 978-1-936096-42-8

Library of Congress Catalogue-in-Publication Data available from the Library of Congress

MANUFACTURED IN CHINA

1 3 5 7 9 10 8 6 4 2

FIRST EDITION

The Heart Truth®, its logo and The Red Dress are registered trademarks of HHS.

Participation by Jimmy Beans Wool does not imply endorsement by HHS/NIH/NHLBI.

Contents

RUFFLED PULLOVER
page 2
❤ *Kim Hargreaves*

SPIRAL RIB COWL
page 6
❤ *Ann Norling*

A-LINE HOODIE
page 22
❤ *Diane Soucy*

L-SHAPED STOLE
page 26
❤ *Barbara Venishnick*

DOLMAN SLEEVE SWEATER
page 43
❤ *Debbie Bliss*

LEAF LACE SWEATER
page 46
❤ *Deborah Newton*

LACE STOLE
page 8
❤ Kieran Foley

LINEN STITCH BLANKET
page 12
❤ Michele Rose Orne

EMBELLISHED CARDIGAN
page 15
❤ Barry Klein

HOME SPA SET
page 19
❤ Jeanne Giles

LACY ANKLETS
page 30
❤ Melissa Morgan-Oakes

BEADED LACE SHAWL
page 32
❤ Andrea Jurgrau

REVERSIBLE WRISTERS
page 36
❤ Kit Hutchin

CABLED CARDI
page 39
❤ Norah Gaughan

LACE INFINITY SCARF
page 52
❤ Tanis Gray

SLIP STITCH BERET
page 54
❤ Ysolda Teague

CABLED KNEE-HIGHS
page 57
❤ Deborah Norville

RED ROSES SHRUG
page 60
❤ Nicky Epstein

GRAPHIC TUNIC
page 64
❤ *Daniela Johannsenova*

MULTIPATTERN MITTENS
page 68
❤ *Jared Flood*

GREENMARKET TOTE
page 72
❤ *Kristin Ashbaugh-Helmreich*

ONE-SHOULDER TUNIC
page 74
❤ *Cornelia Tuttle Hamilton*

LACE HEARTS CARDI
page 77
❤ *Martin Storey*

COWL NECK VEST
page 81
❤ *Cecily Glowik MacDonald*

SNOWBOARDER HAT
page 84
❤ *Lindsey Jacobellis*

SILK AND MOHAIR CAPE
page 87
❤ *Iris Schreier*

HEART MOTIF MITTS
page 90
❤ *Debbie Stoller*

EYELET SHAWL
page 93
❤ *Amy Swenson*

MOHAIR TWIST SWEATER
page 96
❤ *Sarah Hatton*

MODULAR DRESS
page 98
❤ *Maie Landra*

▲ For instructions to make this knit representation of *The Heart Truth* logo, see page 126.

On behalf of the National Heart, Lung, and Blood Institute's *The Heart Truth*® campaign, we are pleased to partner with Jimmy Beans Wool and its innovative Stitch Red program to spread the message about women's heart health and to encourage women to take action to lower their risk factors for heart disease.

The Heart Truth's goal is to give women a personal and urgent wake-up call regarding their own personal risk of heart disease. While this risk starts to rise between the ages of forty and sixty, it is an important message for women of all ages because heart disease can begin at an early age.

We hope that you will share *The Heart Truth*'s key messages wth your friends and family—know your risk factors, get the facts, and incorporate heart-healthy behaviors into your daily life. Remember, it is never too early or too late to take action in preventing and controlling the risk factors for heart disease.

We thank you for your continued support!

Susan B. Shurin, M.D.
Acting Director
National Institutes of Health, National Heart, Lung, and Blood Institute

Crafting for a cause

For as long as I can remember, I've always been making something. I graduated from making clothes for my Barbie dolls to making clothes for myself. Spool knitting took me to "real" knitting. In high school home economics class, when we were told to crochet a pot holder, I made an entire afghan. From my earliest days, I've loved to be able to say "I did it myself." If you're a crafter, you know the feeling. That sense of satisfaction that comes from knowing that if you can knit a scarf or a sweater, well, you can do just about anything! Chances are most of what you make isn't for yourself. You might *think* you're making something for yourself, but often the project turns out so terrific you just have to share it with someone else.

I was delighted to say yes to Laura's request to be a part of *Knit Red*. You'll find plenty of inspiring projects you'll want to make for the people you care about, and that will also keep your crafty engines revved up. And that in turn will keep your most important engine—your heart—working well. Research has shown the repetitive motion of activities like knitting actually has a beneficial cardiac effect, reducing stress hormones and lowering blood pressure and heart rate. It's just as effective as yoga—and, if you ask me, a lot easier! If you have a family history of heart disease, as I do, that's even more reason to keep your needles handy.

If you don't have a family history, you still have a heart, so it's important to know that heart disease is the number-one killer of women in America. Eighty percent of women say they'd call 911 if they thought someone else was having a heart attack, but barely half would call if they thought they were having a heart attack themselves! We women are accustomed to putting everyone else first, but ladies, if we don't take care of ourselves, we won't be here to help the people we love.

This book will help you educate yourself about heart disease and the signs of a heart attack. Learn the important information here about staying healthy. Share what you learn with the women you care about: your sister, your mom, your best friend. Pick a pattern and stitch away, know that while you're "knitting red," you're improving your own health. I get tickled pink just thinking about it!

Deborah Norville

Let's stick it to heart disease!

Thank you for joining Jimmy Beans Wool and all of our friends in the yarn industry in "Sticking It to Heart Disease"! We couldn't be more proud of this book, and we hope that you will enjoy reading it as much as we have enjoyed creating it.

The idea for *Knit Red* was the result of a conversation I had with my friend Marta McGinnis back in 2007. An otherwise healthy marketing executive–turned–sales rep who was barely in her fifties, Marta had recently survived a major heart attack and had subsequently been diagnosed with heart disease. That same year my husband, Doug, an active thirtysomething, had been diagnosed with high blood pressure. Marta and I had both been shocked to learn that heart disease doesn't affect only older men as we had always assumed. In fact, heart disease is the number-one killer of women in the United States and actually kills more American women than all types of cancer combined. As Marta and I shared our stories, we realized that we needed to do something and quickly started putting pen to paper to come up with ideas for a campaign to combat this deadly disease. Tragically, Marta passed away just sixth months after that first meeting. It's obvious to me that we could not have accomplished this project without her support. We miss you, Marta.

Knit Red is one component of the Stitch Red campaign, a partnership between Jimmy Beans Wool and dozens of other companies in the fiber arts industry to raise awareness of heart disease in women. Participating companies have developed products specifically for Stitch Red and are generously donating a portion of the proceeds from sales of the products to the Foundation for the National Institutes of Health in support of *The Heart Truth*®.

We approached some of the brightest stars in the knitting world to design projects for this book and to share their personal experiences with heart disease and tips for heart-healthy living. We were overwhelmed by their generosity and by their stunning designs and inspiring stories. In the following pages, we trust that you will find knitting inspiration, useful information and courage. And we also hope that you will join us by making your own lives more heart healthy. After all, that's what this is all about! ♥

Hugs and many thanks,
Laura Zander (aka Jimmy)

projects and profiles

Ruffled pullover

This tunic-length pullover will flatter any figure.
Delicate ruffled edges give it just a touch of girlish charm.
Keep it casual with jeans or dress it up by pairing
it with a skirt and a beautiful necklace.

KIM'S STORY

British designer Kim's exceptional eye for color and gift for creating garments that appeal to a wide range of individual tastes are a rare combination, and we are so excited to have her as a part of this book. A distinguished designer in the world of handknit fashion, Kim learned to knit and crochet from her mother and grandmother at the early age of five and has been a part of the knitting community virtually her entire life. She enthusiastically agreed to contribute one of her gorgeous designs to *Knit Red* with the hope that it would help encourage knitters to make heart-healthy choices so they can enjoy their craft anytime, anywhere, for a very long time!

KIM'S TIP

EVERYTHING IN
MODERATION!
Kim loves food (perhaps a little too much, she admits) but tries to fill up on fresh foods, like fruits and veggies, to keep her passion for homemade cakes in check.

SIZES

Instructions are written for size X-Small. Changes for Small, Medium, Large, and X-Large are in parentheses. (Shown in size Medium.)

MEASUREMENTS

BUST 40 (42, 44, 46, 48)"/101.5 (106.5, 111.5, 117, 122)cm
LENGTH 28½ (28¾, 29, 29½, 30)"/72.5 (73, 73.5, 75, 76)cm
UPPER ARM 13¼ (13½, 14, 14½, 15)"/33.5 (34, 35.5, 37, 38)cm

MATERIALS

• 7 (8, 9, 9, 9) 1¾oz/50g balls (each approx 153yd/140m) of Rowan *Kid Classic* (lambswool/ kid mohair/nylon) in #847 cherry red (4)
• One pair each sizes 6 and 8 (4 and 5mm) needles *or size to obtain gauge*
• Spare size 6 (4mm) needle
• One size 6 (4mm) circular needle, 29"/75cm long
• Two size 6 (4mm) double-pointed needles (dpns) for I-cord tie

GAUGE

19 sts and 25 rows to 4"/10cm over St st using larger needles.
➤Take time to check gauge.

BACK

With smaller needles, cast on 97 (101, 107, 111, 117) sts. Work in garter st (knit every row) for 4 rows, ending with a WS row. Change to larger needles. Cont in St st (knit on RS, purl on WS) and work even for 38 (40, 40, 42, 42) rows, ending with a WS row.

SIDE SHAPING

Dec row (RS) K1, ssk, k to last 3 sts, k2tog, k1. Rep dec row every 4th row 6 times more, end with a RS row—83 (87, 93, 97, 103) sts. Beg with a purl row, work even for 9 rows, end with a WS row.
Inc row (RS) K1, M1, knit to last st, M1, k1. Rep inc row every 6th row 6 times more—97 (101, 107, 111, 117) sts. Work even until piece measures 19¼ (19½, 19½, 20, 20)"/49 (49.5, 49.5, 51, 51)cm from beg, ending with a WS row.

ARMHOLE SHAPING

Bind off 4 (4, 5, 5, 6) sts at beg of next 2 rows—89 (93, 97, 101, 105) sts.
Dec row 1 (RS) K1, ssk, k to last 3 sts, k2tog, k1.
Dec row 2 (WS) P1, p2tog, p to last 3 sts, p2tog tbl, p1. Rep last 2 rows twice more, then rep dec row 1 every RS row 3 (4, 5, 6, 7) times—71 (73, 75, 77, 79) sts. Work even until armhole measures 8¼ (8¼, 8½, 8½, 9)"/21 (21, 22, 22, 23)cm, end with a WS row.

SHOULDER AND NECK SHAPING

Bind off 8 (8, 8, 8, 9) sts at beg of next 2 rows, 8 sts at beg of next 2 rows, then 7 (7, 8, 8, 8) sts at beg of next 2 rows. AT THE SAME TIME, bind off center 17 (19, 19, 21, 21) sts, then bind off from each neck edge 4 sts once.

FRONT

Work as for back until armhole measures 1"/2.5cm, ending with a WS row. Cont to shape armholes as for back and work neck shaping as foll:

NECK SHAPING

Next row (RS) Work to center st, join a 2nd ball of yarn and bind off center st, work to end. Working both sides at once, and cont to shape armholes as for back, work next WS row.
Next (dec) row (RS) With first ball of yarn, work to last 3 sts, k2tog, k1; with 2nd ball of yarn, k1, ssk, work to end. Cont to dec 1 st from each neck edge every other row 1 (3, 2, 4, 3) time more, then every 4th row 10 (9, 10, 9, 10) times—23 (23, 24, 24, 25) sts each side. Work even until piece measures same as back to shoulder, ending with a WS row.

SHOULDER SHAPING

Bind off 8 (8, 8, 8, 9) sts at beg of next 2 rows, 8 sts at beg of next 2 rows, then 7 (7, 8, 8, 8) sts at beg of next 2 rows.

SLEEVES

FIRST RUFFLE

With smaller needles, cast on 169 (169, 177, 185, 185) sts.

Row 1 (RS) K1, *k2, pass first st over 2nd st; rep from * to end—85 (85, 89, 93, 93) sts.

Row 2 P1, *p2tog, rep from * to end—43 (43, 45, 47, 47) sts. Cont in St st and work even for 12 rows, ending with a WS row. Cut yarn. Leave sts on spare needle.

SECOND RUFFLE

Work rows 1 and 2 as for first ruffle—43 (43, 45, 47, 47) sts. Cont in St st and work even for 8 rows, ending with a WS row. Do not cut yarn.

JOINING RUFFLES

Next (joining) row (RS) With RS facing, place first ruffle sts behind second ruffle sts; *insert 3rd needle knitwise into first st of each needle and wrap yarn around each needle as if to knit, then knit these 2 sts tog and sl them off the needles; rep from * to end—43 (43, 45, 47, 47) sts. Beg with a purl row, cont in St st for 3 rows, ending with a WS row.

Inc row (RS) K1, M1, knit to last st, M1, k1. Rep inc row every 8th row 9 (6, 7, 7, 4) times, then every 6th row 1 (5, 4, 4, 8) time—65 (67, 69, 71, 73) sts. Work even until piece measures 16 (16, 16½, 16½, 16½)"/40.5 (40.5, 42, 42, 42)cm from beg, ending with a WS row.

CAP SHAPING

Bind off 4 (4, 5, 5, 6) sts at beg of next 2 rows—57 (59, 59, 61, 61) sts.

Dec row 1 (RS) K1, ssk, k to last 3 sts, k2tog, k1.

Dec row 2 (WS) P1, p2tog, p to last 3 sts, p2tog tbl, p1—53 (55, 55, 57, 57) sts. Working dec row 1 on RS rows and dec row 2 on

WS rows, cont to dec 1 st each side on next row, then every other row twice more, then every 4th row 5 (5, 6, 6, 7) times. Work next row even. Dec 1 st each side on next row, then every row 3 (4, 3, 4, 3) times more—29 sts. Bind off 4 sts at beg of next 2 rows. Bind off rem 21 sts.

FINISHING

Block pieces to measurements. Sew right shoulder seam.

NECK RUFFLE

With RS facing and circular needle, pick up and k 38 (38, 40, 40, 42) sts evenly spaced along left neck edge, 38 (38, 40, 40, 42) sts along right neck edge, then 25 (27, 27, 29, 29) sts along back neck edge—101 (103, 107, 109, 113) sts.

Row 1 (WS) P61 (63, 65, 67, 69), p2tog tbl, p2tog, purl to end—99 (101, 105, 107, 111) sts.

Row 2 Knit.

Row 3 *P1, M1 p-st; rep from *

to last st, end p1—197 (201, 209, 213, 221) sts.

Row 4 *K1, M1; rep from * to last st, end k1—393 (401, 417, 425, 441) sts.

Bind off knitwise.

Sew left shoulder and neck ruffle seam. Set in sleeves. Sew side and sleeve seams.

I-CORD TIE

With dpn, cast on 4 sts. Work I-cord as foll:

***Next row (RS)** With 2nd dpn, k4, do not turn. Slide sts back to beg of needle to work next row from RS; rep from * until I-cord measures 51 (53, 55, 57, 59)"/129.5 (134.5, 139.5, 145, 150)cm. Cut yarn, leaving an 8"/20.5cm tail. Thread this tail into tapestry needle, then thread through rem sts. Pull tog tightly, secure end, then weave in end. Thread beg tail into tapestry needle, then sew running stitches around top edge. Pull tog tightly to close opening, then secure and weave in end. ❤

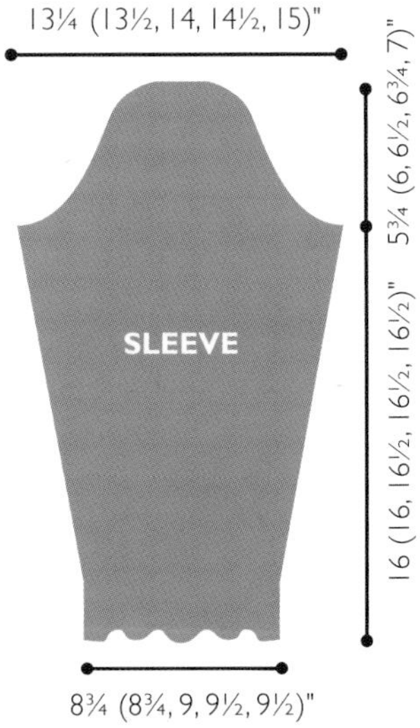

▲ Swap the garter stitch hem for a ruffled edging for a different look.

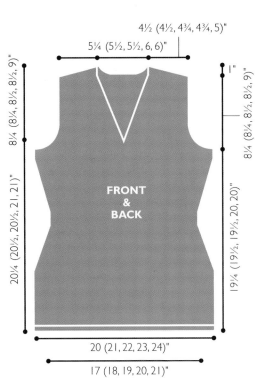

FRONT & BACK

4½ (4½, 4¾, 4¾, 5)"

5¼ (5½, 5½, 6, 6)"

1"

8¼ (8¼, 8½, 8½, 9)"

8¼ (8¼, 8½, 8½, 9)"

20¼ (20½, 20½, 21, 21)"

19¼ (19½, 19½, 20, 20)"

20 (21, 22, 23, 24)"

17 (18, 19, 20, 21)"

SLEEVE

13¼ (13½, 14, 14½, 15)"

5¾ (6, 6½, 6¾, 7)"

16 (16, 16½, 16½, 16½)"

8¾ (8¾, 9, 9½, 9½)"

Spiral rib cowl

The subtle variations in Crystal Palace's *Mochi Plus* yarn emphasize the texture of the rib pattern of this gorgeous neck warmer. Knit this quick project for yourself and for a friend!

SIZE
Instructions are written for one size.

MEASUREMENTS
WIDTH Approx 10"/25.5cm
CIRCUMFERENCE Approx 45"/114.5cm

MATERIALS
• 4 1¾oz/50g balls (each approx 95yd/87m) of Crystal Palace *Mochi Plus* (merino wool/nylon) in #606 red zone (4)
• One size 9 (5.5mm) circular needle, 26"/66cm long *or size to obtain gauge*
• Stitch marker

GAUGE
24 sts and 24 rows to 4"/10cm over spiral rib pat using size 9 (5.5mm) circular needle (unstretched).
➤ Take time to check gauge.

COWL
Cast on 272 sts. Join, taking care not to twist sts on needle, pm for beg of rnds. Cont in spiral rib pat as foll:
Rnds 1–3 *K2, p2; rep from * around.
Rnd 4 *K2, p2; rep from * to 1 st before marker, sl st from LH needle to RH needle, remove marker; sl st on RH needle back to LH needle, then pm for new beg of rnd.
Rep rnds 1–4 for spiral rib pat and work even until piece measures 10"/25.5cm from beg, ending with rnd 3.
Bind off loosely in rib pat.

FINISHING
Block piece lightly to measurements.❤

ANN'S STORY
Ann Norling is actually the "nom de knit" of Marge Okuley, a yarn sales representative in Northern California and Northern Nevada. We love it when Marge visits us at the shop so we can discuss the current yarn trends with her and see her latest designs. Having lost her own father to heart disease, Marge jumped on board with *Knit Red* the moment we approached her. Her father died the day after her 21st birthday, when he was just 60 years old. Marge's friend and colleague Susan Druding, founder of Crystal Palace Yarns, also lost her father to heart disease. Marge thought it apt to design her project for this book using Susan's yarn as a tribute to both of their fathers as well as a united effort to help draw attention to everyone's risk of heart disease.

ANN'S TIP
EATING OUT doesn't mean you have to put your healthy habits on hold. Order your salad with dressing on the side or try sharing an entree with your dinner partner to cut down on oversized portions.

♥ **KIERAN FOLEY**

Lace stole

Whisper-thin yarn knit into an intricate lace pattern creates a sophisticated wrap that is fashionable and timeless.

▬▬▬▬▶

SIZE
Instructions are written for one size.

MEASUREMENTS
Approx 25½" x 56"/64.5 x 142cm

MATERIALS
• 3 1¾oz/50g balls (each approx 440yd/403m) of Classic Elite Yarns *Silky Alpaca Lace* (alpaca/silk) in #2432 garnet ⓪
• Size 4 (3.5mm) circular needle, 32"/81cm long, *or size to obtain gauge*

GAUGE
20 sts and 26 rows to 4"/10cm over chart pats using size 4 (3.5mm) circular needle (after blocking).
➤ Take time to check gauge.

NOTE
WS rows are not shown on charts. Purl all WS rows.

KIERAN'S STORY
At Jimmy Beans, we are all big fans of Kieran's innovative work with lace and stranded colorwork, which he often combines to stunning effect. When he agreed to be a part of *Knit Red* (his first book project), we couldn't have been more thrilled! Kieran hopes that knitters everywhere will use this book not only as a source for creative inspiration, but as a guide to improving their overall well-being. Kieran doesn't have a car and stays fit by riding his bike to get from place to place in his hometown of Dublin, Ireland. He also relies on his workout buddy—his dog—to keep him plenty active.

♥ **KIERAN'S TIP**
IT'S BEST TO KEEP PROCESSED FOODS TO A MINIMUM, but when you do indulge, be sure to check the ingredients list for trans fats, excess sodium, and other unhealthy components.

STOLE
Cast on 129 sts. Knit 2 rows.

BEG CHART PAT 1
Row 1 (RS) Work first st, work 28-st rep 4 times, then work last 16 sts.
Row 2 and all WS rows Purl. Cont to foll chart in this way to row 17; st count will inc to 157 sts.
Row 18 Purl.

BEG CHART PAT 2
Row 1 (RS) Work first st, work 35-st rep 4 times, then work last 16 sts.
Row 2 and all WS rows Purl. Cont to foll chart in this way to row 11; st count will inc to 161 sts, then dec back to 157 sts.
Row 12 Purl. Cont to rep rows 1–12 twenty-six times more, ending with a WS row.

CHART 3

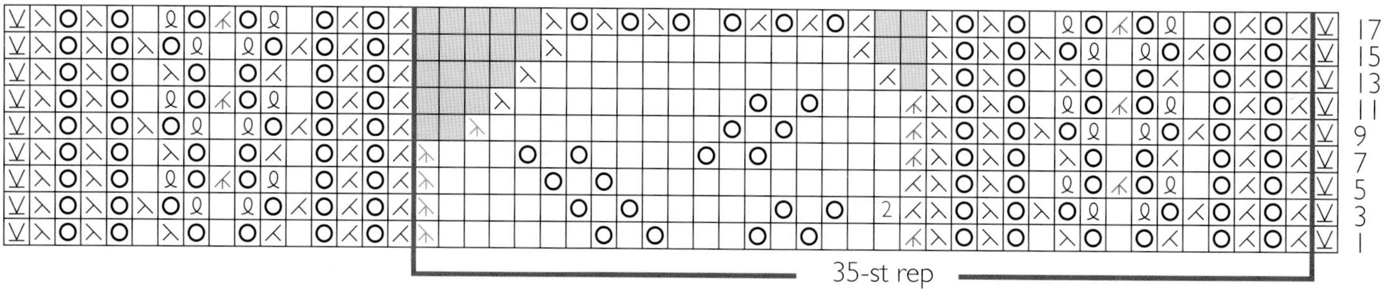

17
15
13
11
9
7
5
3
1
35-st rep

CHART 2

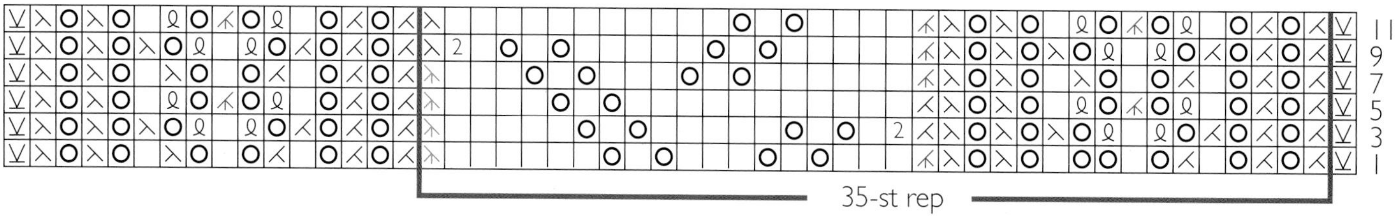

11
9
7
5
3
1
35-st rep

CHART 1

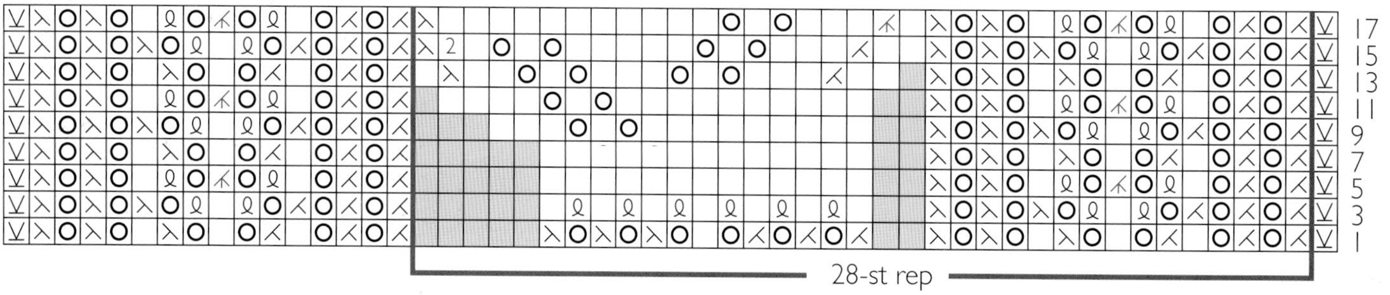

17
15
13
11
9
7
5
3
1
28-st rep

BEG CHART PAT 3

Row 1 (RS) Work first st, work 35-st rep 4 times, work last 16 sts.

Row 2 and all WS rows Purl.

Cont to foll chart in this way to row 17; st count will dec to 129 sts.

Row 18 Purl. Knit 3 rows.

Bind off all sts loosely knitwise.

FINISHING

Block piece to measurements.

STITCH KEY

- Knit
- K1 tbl
- K2
- K2tog
- Ssk
- K3tog
- K3tog tbl
- Sl st purlwise wy
- Yarn over
- No stitch

Linen stitch blanket

With a stitch pattern that mimics the look of woven fabric and subtle color play, this sumptuous blanket is reminiscent of the blankets Swans Island is renowned for.

■■■▭

MEASUREMENTS
Approx 48" x 64½"/122cm x 164cm

MATERIALS
• 6 3½oz/100g hanks (each approx 525yd/480m) of Swans Island *Natural Colors Fingering Weight* (organic merino wool) in #YF120 winterberry (A) 🔟
• 4 skeins in #YF101 garnet (B)
• 1 3½oz/100g skein (each approx 525yd/480m) of Swans Island *Pure Blends Fingering Weight* (organic merino wool/alpaca) in #YF110 oatmeal (C) 🔟
• Size 11 (8mm) circular needle, 36"/91cm long, *or size to obtain gauge*

GAUGE
28 sts to 5"/12.5cm and 40 rows to 4"/10cm over linen st using 2 strands of yarn held tog and size 11 (8mm) circular needle.
➤Take time to check gauge.

NOTES
1) Use 2 strands of yarn held tog.
2) For color D, use 1 strand A and 1 strand B held tog.
3) Center of blanket is worked vertically from side edge (cast-on) to side edge (bind-off).
4) Borders are picked up and worked horizontally.

LINEN STITCH
(over a multiple of 2 sts plus 1)
Row 1 (RS) Sl 1 purlwise wyif, *k1, sl 1 purlwise wyif; rep from * to end.
Row 2 P1, *sl 1 purlwise wyib, p1; rep from * to end.
Rep rows 1 and 2 for linen st.

BLANKET
CENTER
With D (1 strand each of A and B held tog), cast on 277 sts. Purl next row. Work in linen st with selvage sts and stripe pat as foll:
Row 1 (RS) Sl 1 tbl wyib, sl 1 purlwise wyif, *k1, sl 1 purlwise wyif; rep from * to last st, end k1 tbl.

Row 2 Sl 1 tbl wyif, p1, *sl 1 purlwise wyib, p1; rep from * to last st, end p1 tbl.
Rep rows 1 and 2 for linen st with selvage sts. Work even until piece measures 4½"/11.5cm from beg, end with a WS row.
Cont in stripe pat as foll:
Next row (RS) Change to B. Work even for 6"/15cm, end with a WS row. Piece should measure 10½"/26.5cm from beg.
Next row (RS) Change to D. Work even for 3½"/9cm, end with a WS row. Piece should measure 14"/35.5cm from beg.
Next row (RS) Change to A. Work even for 20"/51cm. Piece should measure 34"/86.5cm from beg.
Next row (RS) Change to D. Work even for 3½"/9cm, end with a WS row. Piece should measure 37½"/95cm from beg.
Next row (RS) Change to B. Work even for 6"/15cm, end with a WS row. Piece should measure 43½"/110.5cm from beg.
Next row (RS) Change to D. Work even for 4½"/11.5cm, end with a WS row. Piece should measure 48"/122cm from beg. Bind off knitwise.

FIRST BORDER
With RS of center facing and D, pick up and k 269 sts evenly spaced along RH selvage st edge. Purl next row. Work in linen st with selvage sts as foll:

MICHELE'S TIP

TEAMWORK WORKS!
If you're having trouble staying motivated to exercise on a regular basis, try finding a buddy to work out or walk with. Make it a regular appointment and you can help to keep each other on track.

Row 1 (RS) Sl 1 tbl wyib, sl 1 purlwise wyif, *k1, sl 1 purlwise wyif; rep from * to last st, end k1 tbl.

Row 2 Sl 1 tbl wyif, p1, *sl 1 purlwise wyib, p1; rep from * to last st, end p1 tbl.

Rep rows 1 and 2 for linen st with selvage sts. Work even 8 rows more, end with a WS row. Cont in stripe pat as foll:

Next row (RS) Change to C. Work even for 2 rows.

Next row (RS) Change to D. Work even for 4 rows.

Next row (RS) Change to C. Work even for 6 rows.

Next row (RS) Change to D. Work even for 4 rows.

Next row (RS) Change to C. Work even for 2 rows.

Next row (RS) Change to A. Work even for 2"/5cm, end with a WS row.

Next row (RS) Change to B. Work even for 1"/2.5cm, end with a WS row.

Next row (RS) Change to C. Work even for 1"/2.5cm, end with a WS row. Border should measure approx 7½"/19cm. Bind off knitwise.

SECOND BORDER
Work same as first border on LH selvage st edge.

FINISHING
Block piece to measurements. ❤

Embellished cardigan

A simple structure is anything but plain when knit in a drop-stitch and stripes pattern, edged in crochet, and adorned with ruffles made of a unique mesh yarn.

SIZES

Instructions are written for size Small. Changes for Medium and Large are in parentheses. (Shown in size Small.)

MEASUREMENTS

BUST (closed) 35 (40½, 46)"/ 89 (103, 117)cm
LENGTH (including edging) 24½ (25, 25½)"/62 (63.5, 64.5)cm
UPPER ARM 13 (14, 15)"/33 (35.5, 38)cm

MATERIALS

• 5 (6, 7) 1¾oz/50g balls (each approx 136yd/124m) of Trendsetter *Merino 6* (merino wool) in #2029 wine (A) ⓷

• 4 (5, 6) .7oz/20g balls (each approx 90yd/82m) of Trendsetter *Charm* (polyamide/Tactel nylon) in #1477 red raspberries (B) ⓺

• 4 (5, 6) 1¾oz/50g balls (each approx 80yd/73m) of Trendsetter *Dune* (mohair/nylon/acrylic) in #91 red blaze (C) ⓸

• 1 3½oz/100g ball (approx 33yd/32m) of Trendsetter *Poppy* (acrylic/wool/cotton) in #6 red barron ⓸

• One pair each sizes 8 and 9 (5 and 5.5mm) needles *or size to obtain gauge*

• Size F/5 (3.75mm) crochet hook

• Three ¾"/19mm buttons
• Dark maroon sewing thread
• Sewing needles

GAUGE

16 sts and 21 rows to 4"/10cm over drop-st pat and stripe pat using larger needles.
➤ Take time to check gauge.

DROP-STITCH PATTERN

[Over a multiple of 7 (8, 9) sts plus 6 (7, 8)]
Row 1 (RS) Purl.
Rows 2 and 4 Knit.
Rows 3 and 5 Purl.
Row 6 (WS) *K 6 (7, 8), drop next st off LH needle and unravel it 4 rows down, so there are 4 loose strands behind st, insert RH needle from front into 5th st

BARRY'S STORY

Barry, the creative genius behind Trendsetter Yarns, always keeps us guessing what the next trend in fashion-forward yarn and knitwear design will be each season. We are honored to have his expertise in contemporary style, and his insights into heart disease, included in *Knit Red!* Barry observed the damaging effects of heart disease in his grandmother, who not only suffered from heart disease, but also underwent quadruple bypass surgery and had a stroke. Barry has committed to making significant changes to his own eating habits and fitness. A few years ago he joined Weight Watchers, which taught him how to control the amount of fat, sodium, and sugar he consumed and that maintaining a healthy lifestyle is all about enjoying what you eat and how you live, not feeling like you are on a diet. While you can't just wave a wand and magically be healthy, Barry points out that taking the time to invest in your physical well-being directly improves your overall quality of life, so stick with those healthy choices!

▲ For a more casual look, you can leave off the ruffles.

down and also under the 4 loose strands, then knit, drawing the st up and catching strands behind it; rep from *, end k 6 (7, 8).
Rep rows 1–6 for drop-st pat.

STRIPE PATTERN
Working in drop-st pat, *work 1 row B, 1 row C, and 1 row A; rep from * (3 rows) for stripe pat.

K1, P1 RIB
(over a multiple of 2 sts plus 1)
Row 1 (RS) K1, *p1, k1; rep from * to end.
Row 2 P1, *k1, p1; rep from * to end.
Rep rows 1 and 2 for k1, p1 rib.

BACK
With larger needles and A, cast on 76 (87, 98) sts. Cont in drop-st pat and stripe pat, work even until piece measures 2"/5cm from beg, ending with a WS row.

SIDE SHAPING
Dec 1 st each side on next row, then every 6th row 7 times more—60 (71, 82) sts. Work even until piece measures 12"/30.5cm from beg, ending with a WS row. Working new sts into drop-st pat, inc 1 st each side on next row, then every 4th row 4 times more—70 (81, 92) sts. Work even until piece measures 16½"/42cm from beg, ending with a WS row.

ARMHOLE SHAPING
Bind off 4 (5, 6) sts at beg of next 2 rows—62 (71, 80) sts. Dec 1 st each side on next row, then every other row 5 (7, 9) times more—50 (55, 60) sts. Work even until armhole measures 7½ (8, 8½)"/19 (20.5, 21.5)cm, ending with a WS row. Bind off all sts purlwise.

LEFT FRONT
With larger needles and A, cast on 41 (47, 53) sts. Cont in drop-st pat and stripe pat, work even

♥ **BARRY'S TIP**
IT CAN BE DIFFICULT TO FIND TIME FOR REGULAR EXERCISE. Barry, who travels nonstop, runs a company, knits, and designs, makes an effort to set aside at least one day each week for mandatory workout time. It's easier if it's fun. Go for a hike, challenge a friend to a game of tennis, or enroll in an aerobics class!

until piece measures 2"/5cm from beg, ending with a WS row.

SIDE SHAPING
Dec 1 st at beg of next row, then at same edge every 6th row 7 times more—33 (39, 45) sts. Work even until piece measures 12"/30.5cm from beg, ending with a WS row. Working new sts into drop-st pat, inc 1 st at beg of next row, then at same edge every 4th row 4 times more—38 (44, 50) sts. Work even until piece measures 15½"/39.5cm from beg, ending with a WS row.

NECK SHAPING
Dec 1 st at end of next row, then at same edge every other row 11 (12, 13) times more, then every 4th row 4 times. AT THE SAME TIME, when piece measures 16½"/42cm from beg, end with a WS row.

ARMHOLE SHAPING
Bind off 4 (5, 6) sts at beg of next row. Work next row even. Dec 1 st from armhole edge on next row, then every other row 5 (7, 9) times more. When all shaping has been completed, work even in 12 (14, 16) sts until piece measures same length as back to shoulder, ending with a WS row. Bind off all sts purlwise.

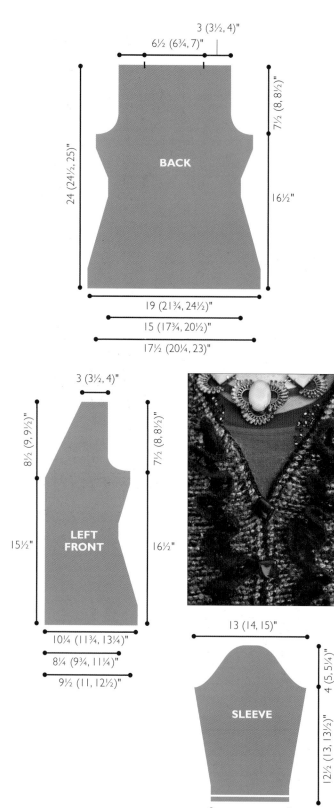

BACK

3 (3½, 4)"
6½ (6¾, 7)"
7½ (8, 8½)"
24 (24½, 25)"
16½"
19 (21¾, 24½)"
15 (17¾, 20½)"
17½ (20¼, 23)"

LEFT FRONT

3 (3½, 4)"
8½ (9, 9½)"
7½ (8, 8½)"
15½"
16½"
10¼ (11¾, 13¼)"
8¼ (9¾, 11¼)"
9½ (11, 12½)"

SLEEVE

13 (14, 15)"
4 (5, 5¼)"
12½ (13, 13½)"
9 (9½, 10)"

RIGHT FRONT

Work same as left front, reversing all shaping.

SLEEVES

With smaller needles and A, cast on 41 (43, 45) sts. Work in k1, p1 rib for 6 rows, dec 7 (4, 1) sts evenly spaced across last row, and end with a WS row—34 (39, 44) sts. Change to larger needles. Cont in drop-st pat and stripe pat until piece measures 2"/5cm from beg, ending with a WS row. Working new sts into drop-st pat, inc 1 st each side on next row, then every 6th row 7 (6, 1) times more, then every 8th row 1 (2, 6) time—52 (57, 60) sts. Work even until piece measures 12½ (13, 13½)"/31.5 (33, 34)cm from beg, end with a WS row.

CAP SHAPING

Bind off 4 (5, 6) sts at beg of next 2 rows—44 (47, 48) sts. Dec 1 st each side on next row, then every other row 9 (10, 11) times more, ending with a WS row—24 (25, 24) sts. Bind off 3 sts at beg of next 4 rows. Bind off rem 12 (13, 12) sts purlwise.

FINISHING

Block pieces lightly to measurements. Sew shoulder seams. Set in sleeves. Sew side and sleeve seams. Place markers for 3 buttonholes along right front edge, with the first 9½"/24cm from lower edge, the last at beg of neck shaping, and the other evenly spaced between.

EDGING

With RS facing and crochet hook, join A with a sl st in bottom edge of right side seam.
Rnd 1 (RS) Ch 1, making sure that work lies flat, sc evenly around entire outer edge, working 3 sc in each corner, using C, join rnd with a sl st in first sc.

Rnd 2 (RS) Ch 1, sc in each st around, working 2 sc in each corner st, using A, join rnd with a sl st in first sc. Cut C.
Rnd (buttonhole) 3 (RS) Ch 1, sc in each st to first marker, [ch 3, skip next 2 sts, sc in each st to next marker] 3 times, cont to sc in each st around, join rnd with a sl st in first sc. Fasten off.

RUFFLES

Working from ball of D, reel off about 2yd/2m of yarn; do not cut. Fan out yarn to separate the mesh. Fold bottom edge of mesh twice to one side, so fanned out yarn measures approx 1½"/4cm wide. Working from RS to WS, insert 1"/2.5cm end of yarn through first drop-st opening in RH vertical column of drop-sts next to front edge of right front. Fold yarn end up, then use sewing needle and thread to secure end in place. Leave this needle on WS. On RS, use second needle and thread to sew running sts through double layer of mesh for approx 1yd/1m. Pull thread to gather in and create ruffles. Pin gathers to column of sts, then sew in place from WS using first needle and thread. Cont to work in this manner to last drop-st opening. Cut yarn, leaving a 1"/2.5cm end. Insert end through last drop-st opening. Fold end down, then secure end in place. For second ruffle, skip next vertical column of sts to left of first ruffle. For third ruffle, skip next vertical column to left of second ruffle. Work ruffles on left front. For each sleeve, gather and sew a 4"/10cm long row of ruffles in each vertical column of drop-sts, then in sleeve seam. Sew on buttons. ❤

♥ JEANNE GILES

Home spa set

Pamper yourself (and lower your stress!) with this collection of bath-time accessories. Knit another set for a friend who could use a little extra TLC.

NOTE Yarn amounts are given for individual projects. To make all three projects, you will need two balls of yarn.

TWISTED RIB

(over an even number of sts)
Row 1 (RS) *K1 tbl, p1;
rep from * to end.
Row 2 *K1, p1 tbl;
rep from * to end.
Rep rows 1 and 2 for twisted rib.

ROSETTE STITCH

(over an even number of sts)
Row 1 (RS) *K2tog, leaving sts on LH needle, p2tog in same st, sl sts to RH needle; rep from * to end.
Row 2 Purl.
Row 3 K1, *k2tog, leaving sts on LH needle, p2tog in same st, sl sts to RH needle; rep from *, end k1.
Row 4 Purl.
Rep rows 1–4 for rosette st.

FACE CLOTH

MEASUREMENTS
Approx 8¾"/22cm wide × 8½"/21.5cm long

MATERIALS
• 1 1¾oz/50g ball (each approx 146yd/135m) of Tahki *Cotton Classic Lite* (mercerized cotton) in #4995 deepest red (3)
• One pair size 6 (4mm) needles *or size to obtain gauge*
• Size E/4 (3.5mm) crochet hook
• Stitch markers

GAUGE

36 sts and 36 rows to 4"/10cm over rosette st using size 6 (4mm) needles (after blocking).

➤ Take time to check gauge.

FACE CLOTH

Cast on 54 sts. Work in twisted rib for 2 rows, ending with a WS row. **Next row (RS)** Work in twisted rib over first 2 sts, pm, work in rosette st over next 50 sts, pm, work in twisted rib over last 2 sts. Keeping 2 sts each side in twisted rib and rem sts in rosette st, work even until piece measures 7½"/19cm from beg, ending with row 3 of rosette st. **Next row (WS)** Work row 2 of twisted rib across, dropping markers. **Next row** Work row 1 of twisted rib. Bind off knitwise.

EDGING

With WS facing and crochet hook, join yarn with a sl st in any corner. **Rnd 1** Ch 1, making sure that work lies flat, sc evenly around entire edge, working 2 sc in each corner; join rnd with a sl st in first sc. Fasten off.

FINISHING

Block piece to measurements. ❤

SOAP COZY

SIZE

Instructions are written for one size.

MEASUREMENTS

Approx 6"/15cm wide x 5½"/14cm long

MATERIALS

• 1 1¾oz/50g ball (each approx 146yd/135m) of Tahki *Cotton Classic Lite* (mercerized cotton) in #4995 deepest red
• One set (5) size 6 (4mm) double-pointed needles (dpns) *or size to obtain gauge*

• 19"/48cm length of white cotton butcher's twine

GAUGE

20 sts and 32 rnds to 4"/10cm over twisted rib using size 6 (4mm) needles (after blocking).

➤ Take time to check gauge.

SOAP COZY

Beg at top edge, cast on 30 sts for picot edge as foll: using the knit cast-on method, *cast on 5 sts; bind off 2 sts; sl first st on RH needle back to LH needle; rep from * until 30 sts have been cast on. Divide sts over 4 needles. Joining taking care not to twist sts on needles, pm for beg of rnds. Cont to work eyelets as foll:
Rnd 1 *K2tog, yo; rep from * around.
Rnd 2 *Yo, k2tog; rep from * around.
Rnds 3 and 4 Knit.
Rnd 5 *K2tog, yo; rep from * around.
Rnds 6 and 7 Knit. Cont to work in twisted rib until piece measures approx 5½"/14cm from beg. Cut yarn, leaving a 10"/25.5cm tail. Divide sts evenly between 2 needles. Graft sts using Kitchener st to close bottom opening.

FINISHING

Block piece to measurements. Thread cotton twine through rnd 5 of eyelets. ❤

> ❤ **JEANNE'S TIP**
> ALWAYS CHECK THE NUTRITION FACTS ON PACKAGED FOODS, read the ingredients, and try to avoid buying and consuming foods that have ingredients you cannot pronounce. Chances are, if you can't say it, you shouldn't eat it!

SPA MITT

SIZE

Instructions are written for one size.

MEASUREMENTS

HAND CIRCUMFERENCE
8"/20.5cm
LENGTH OF CUFF
2"/5cm

MATERIALS

• 2 1¾oz/50g balls (each approx 146yd/135m) of Tahki *Cotton Classic Lite* (mercerized cotton) in #4995 deepest red
• One set (5) each sizes 6 and 7 (4 and 4.5mm) double-pointed needles (dpns) *or size to obtain gauge*
• Stitch marker

GAUGE

20 sts and 20 rnds to 4"/10cm over rosette st using 2 strands held tog and smaller dpn (after blocking).

➤ Take time to check gauge.

NOTE

Use 2 strands of yarn held tog throughout.

SPA MITT

With smaller dpns, and 2 strands of yarn held tog, cast on 40 sts. Divide sts over 4 needles. Join, taking care not to twist sts on needles, pm for beg of rnds. Work around in twisted rib for 2"/5cm. Change to larger dpns. Cont in rosette st until piece measures 9½"/24cm from beg, ending with rnd 3. Cut yarn, leaving a 10"/25.5cm tail. Divide sts evenly between 2 needles. Graft sts using Kitchener st to close top opening.

FINISHING

Block piece to measurements. ❤

A-line hoodie

This swingy cardigan is the perfect cover-up to slip into when you're on the go. The drawstring hood and two-button closure update the classic look.

◀■■■▭

SIZES

Instructions are written for size X-Small. Changes for Small, Medium, Large, X-Large, and XX-Large are in parentheses. (Shown in size X-Small.)

MEASUREMENTS

BUST (closed) approx 33 (37, 41, 45, 49, 53)"/84 (94, 104, 114, 124.5, 134.5)cm
LENGTH 26 (26½, 27, 27½, 28, 29)"/66 (67.5, 68.5, 70, 71, 73.5)cm
UPPER ARM 13½ (15, 17, 18½, 19, 20½)"/34 (38, 43, 47, 48, 52)cm

MATERIALS

• 17 (17, 18, 20, 23, 26) 1¾ oz/50g balls (each approx 93yd/85m) of Universal Yarn/Debbie Macomber Blossom Street Collection *Cashmere Fleur de Lys* (merino wool/cashmere) in #416 courage (4)
• Size 8 (5mm) circular needles, 29"/75cm and 16"/40cm long *or size to obtain gauge*
• One set (5) size 8 (5mm) double-pointed needles (dpns)
• Size 6 (4mm) circular needle, 29"/75cm long
• One set (5) size 6 (4mm) double-pointed needles (dpns)
• Stitch holders or waste yarn
• Stitch markers
• Small safety pins
• Three 1"/25mm buttons

GAUGE

18 sts and 25 rows to 4"/10cm over St st using size 8 (5mm) needles.
➤ Take time to check gauge.

SEED STITCH

(over multiple of 2 sts)
Row 1 (RS) *K1, p1; rep from * to end.
Row 2 Purl the knit sts and knit the purl sts.
Rep row 2 for seed st.

NOTE

Cardigan is worked in one piece from the top down; hood is worked after.

CARDIGAN

YOKE
With longer size 8 (5mm) needle, cast on 2 sts (front), pm, cast on 10 (10, 8, 8, 8, 8) sts (sleeve), pm, cast on 24 (26, 28, 30, 34, 36) sts (back), pm, cast on 10 (10, 8, 8, 8, 8) sts (sleeve), pm, cast on 2 sts (front)—48 (50, 48, 50, 54, 56) sts.
Row 1 (RS) *Knit to 1 st before marker, kfb, slip marker, kfb; rep from * across, knit to end—8 sts inc.
Row 2 Purl.
Rows 3 and 4 Rep rows 1 and 2—64 (66, 64, 66, 70, 72) sts.
Row 5 K2, M1, *knit to 1 st

DIANE'S STORY

Although never an official staff member, Diane has been a member of the Jimmy Beans family since the beginning. From helping us pick out which yarns we should carry in our shop to answering the JBW help hotline, she's been an integral part of the business. We didn't have to ask Diane twice to create a design for this book to help us raise awareness of heart disease. Diane's mother suffered from a rheumatic heart and had a pacemaker for over 20 years, and Diane knows just how much of a difference diet and exercise can make in maintaining one's quality of life. Diane herself has a heart murmur, which isn't a big deal, she tells us, but she makes an effort to visit her doctor regularly to ensure she is in tip-top shape for knitting, designing, and playing with her pups and grandkids!

♥ **DIANE'S TIP**
WHEN DIANE GOES OUT TO EAT, she likes to make healthy choices by selecting foods cooked in heart-healthy ways. She suggests looking for terms such as *broiled, baked, roasted, poached,* or *lightly sautéed.*

before marker, kfb, slip marker, kfb; rep from * across, knit to last 2 sts, M1, k2—10 sts inc.

Row 6 Purl.

Rep last 2 rows until there are 34 (38, 40, 44, 48, 50) sts between the back markers. On last 2 rows, cast on 10 (11, 12, 12, 14, 16) sts at beg of next 2 rows. Rep rows 1 and 2, working first and last 10 sts in seed st throughout, twice.

Next (buttonhole) row (RS)

Work in pat to last 5 sts, bind off 2 sts, work to end. On next row, cast on 2 sts over bound-off sts. Cont to rep rows 1 and 2 until there are 66 (74, 80, 88, 96, 104) sts between the back markers. At the same time, make 2 more buttonholes, each 3"/7.5cm from the previous one—246 (276, 292, 320, 340, 374) total sts. Piece measures approx 6¾ (7½, 8½, 9¼, 10, 10¾)"/17 (19, 21.5, 23.5, 25.5, 27.5)cm.
End with a WS row.

DIVIDE FOR SLEEVES

Next row (RS) Work in pat across 38 (43, 46, 50, 52, 59) front sts, place next 52 (58, 60, 66, 70, 76) sleeve sts on a holder, cast on 7 (8, 11, 12, 13, 14) sts at underarm, knit across 66 (74, 80, 88, 96, 104) back sts, place next 52 (58, 60, 66, 70, 76) sleeve sts on a holder, cast on 7 (8, 11, 12, 13, 14) sts at underarm, work in pat to end—156 (176, 194, 212, 226, 250) body sts.

BODY

Work in St st with first and last 10 sts in seed st as set until piece measures 13 (13, 14, 14, 16, 17)"/33 (33, 35.5, 35.5, 40.5, 43)cm from beg, ending with a WS row.

Next (inc) row (RS) Work in seed st over first 10 sts, k1 (0, 2, 0, 1, 0), *k3 (3, 4, 4, 5, 5), M1; rep from * to 10 sts before end of row, work in seed st to end—201 (228, 237, 260, 267, 296) sts. Work even until piece measures 25 (25½, 26, 26½, 27, 28)"/63.5 (65, 66, 67.5, 68.5, 71)cm from beg. Work in seed st for 1"/2.5cm. Bind off.

HOOD

With smaller 29"/73.5cm circular needle, cast on 4 sts. With RS facing, pick up and knit 18 (19, 21, 21, 23, 24) sts across front; 10 (10, 8, 8, 8, 8) sts across top of the sleeve; 24 (26, 28, 30, 32, 34) sts across back of the neck; 10 (10, 8, 8, 8, 8) sts across top of sleeve; and 18 (19, 21, 21, 23, 24) sts across front; cast on 4 sts—88 (92, 94, 96, 102, 106) sts. (4 sts at each end of row forms the casing).

Next row (WS) Purl.

Next row K3, sl 1, knit to last 4 sts, sl 1, k3.

Rep last 2 rows until hood measures 12"/30.5cm, ending with a RS row.

Next row P44 (46, 47, 48, 51, 53), pm, purl to end.

Next (dec) row (RS) K3, sl 1, knit to 6 sts before marker, [k2tog] twice, k2, slip marker, k2, [ssk] twice, knit to 4 sts before end of row, sl 1, k3—4 sts dec.

Next row Purl. Rep last 2 rows once, then rep dec row once more—8 sts dec. Bind off. Fold in half and sew top seam closed.

SLEEVES

Place 52 (58, 60, 66, 70, 76) held sleeve sts on 16"/40.5cm circular needle. Join yarn and pick up and knit 10 (11, 14, 15, 16, 17) sts along underarm, pm approx in center of underarm sts to mark beg of rnd—62 (69, 74, 81, 86, 93) sts. Knit 3 rnds.

Next (dec) rnd K1, ssk, knit to last 3 sts, k2tog, k1—2 sts dec.

Cont in St st, rep dec rnd every 6th (6th, 5th, 4th, 4th, 3rd) rnd 10 (12, 14, 16, 18, 20) times—40 (43, 44, 47, 48, 51) sts, changing to larger dpns when necessary. Work even until sleeve measures 17½ (17, 17, 16½, 16½, 15½)"/44.5 (43, 43, 42, 42, 39.5)cm. Work in seed st for 3"/7.5cm more. Bind off.

FINISHING

Block pieces to measurements. Stitch edge of casing down on WS of hood. If desired, thread casing with a twisted cord, crocheted cord, or I-cord measuring approx 34"/86.5cm. Weave in ends. Sew buttons opposite buttonholes. ❤

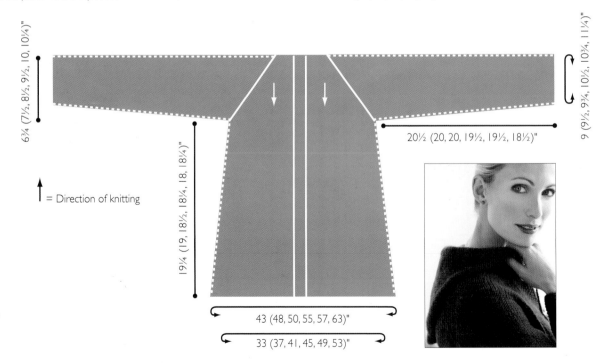

6¾ (7½, 8½, 9½, 10, 10¼)"

9 (9½, 9¾, 10½, 10¾, 11¼)"

20½ (20, 20, 19½, 19½, 18½)"

▲ = Direction of knitting

19¼ (19, 18½, 18¼, 18, 18¼)"

43 (48, 50, 55, 57, 63)"

33 (37, 41, 45, 49, 53)"

L-shaped stole

This lightweight wrap consists of two rectangles, knit separately and sewn to form a V. Originally designed for *Vogue® Knitting* in a palette of neutrals, it gets a new life in vivid reds.

◀■■■▭

SIZE
Instructions are written
for one size.

MEASUREMENTS
Approx 16½/42cm wide ×
49"/124.5cm long
(including all trims)

MATERIALS
• 7 1¾oz/50g balls (each approx
109yd/97m) of Classic Elite Yarns
Inca Alpaca (alpaca) in #1153
damask red (A) (**4**)
• 6 balls in #1158 rio red (B)
• One pair size 5 (3.75mm)
needles *or size to obtain gauge*
• Size 5 (3.75mm) circular
needle, 32"/81cm long

GAUGE
21 sts and 32 rows to
4"/10cm over pat st using
size 5 (3.75mm) needles.
➤Take time to check gauge.

BARBARA'S STORY
Taught by her mother (who
learned from her mother),
Barbara first picked up knitting
needles at the age of five. This
early introduction to fiber arts
turned into a lifelong passion.
After receiving an art degree,
Barbara worked as a textile
and fabric designer, putting her
career on hold to raise a
family. After her children were
grown, Barbara took a job at a
local yarn shop and began
teaching classes and
workshops, before eventually
turning her attention to
design. A frequent contributor
to *Vogue Knitting* and other
major knitting publications,
Barbara became a member of
the Professional Designers
Guild on 1995. In 2005, at the
age of 56, Barbara died
suddenly of a heart attack. We
included one of her most
popular designs in *Knit Red* to
honor this innovative designer
and remarkable woman.

SHAWL
LONG RECTANGLE
With straight needles and A,
cast on 81 sts. Work next 3
preparation rows as foll:
Preparation row 1 (WS) Purl.
Preparation row 2 (RS) Knit.
Preparation row 3 (WS) P2, *p1
wrapping yarn twice around
needle, p3; rep from *, end last
rep p2 (instead of p3).

BEG PAT ST
Row 1 (RS) With B, k2, *sl 1 wyib
dropping extra wrap, k1, insert
RH needle into next st of 2 rows
below and knit it, k1; rep from *,
end last rep k2 (instead of k3).
Row 2 With B, p2, *sl 1 wyif, p3;
rep from *, end last rep p2
(instead of p3).
Row 3 With B, knit.
Row 4 With B, p2, *p1 wrapping

yarn twice around needle, p1, p3; rep from *, end last rep p2 (instead of p3).

Rows 5–8 With A, rep rows 1–4.
Rep rows 1–8 for pat st and stripe pat. Work even until piece measures 48"/122cm from beg, ending with row 3.

SHORT EDGE TRIM
Next row (WS) With A, *k3, k2tog, k4; rep from * 8 times more—72 sts.
Next row (RS) Purl.
Next row (WS) Knit. Bind off all sts purlwise.

SHORT RECTANGLE
Work same as long rectangle until piece measures 32½"/82.5cm from beg, end with row 3. Work short edge trim.

FINISHING
Block pieces lightly to measurements on diagram. Referring to diagram, sew cast-on edge of short rectangle to RH edge of long rectangle.

FIRST LONG EDGE TRIM
With RS facing, circular needle and A, beg in row below short edge trim of long rectangle and pick up and k 1 st in every other row along entire LH edge.
K1 row, p1 row, k1 row.
Bind off all sts purlwise.

SECOND LONG EDGE TRIM
With RS facing, circular needle and A, beg in cast-on row of long rectangle and pick up and k 1 st in every other st to seam, then pick up and k 1 st in every other row along RH edge of short rectangle to short edge trim.
K1 row, p1 row, k1 row.
Bind off all sts purlwise.

THIRD LONG EDGE TRIM
With RS facing, circular needle and A, beg in row below short edge trim of short rectangle and pick up and k 1 st in every other row along LH edge to seam.
K1 row, p1 row, k1 row. Bind off all sts purlwise.

FOURTH LONG EDGE TRIM
With RS facing, circular needle and A, beg at seam and pick up and k 1 st in every other row along RH edge of long rectangle to short edge trim. K1 row, p1 row, k1 row. Bind off all sts purlwise. Sew ends of trims tog at outer corners and inner corner. ♥

↑ = Direction of work

15½"

½"

LONG RECTANGLE

LH edge

RH edge

48"

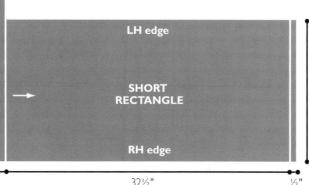

LH edge

SHORT RECTANGLE

RH edge

15½"

15½"

32½"

½"

MELISSA MORGAN-OAKES

Lacy anklets

These flirty socks are worked from the top down in a pretty eyelet pattern. The alpaca-wool-blend yarn pampers the feet.

◀■■□

SIZE
Instructions are written for size Medium.

MEASUREMENTS
CIRCUMFERENCE (unstretched) 6"/15cm (fits up to 9"/23cm)

MATERIALS
• 1 3½oz/100g ball (each approx 450yd/411m) of Classic Elite Yarns *Alpaca Sox Solids* (alpaca/wool/nylon) in #1832 Cereza (**1**)
• Size 1 (2.25mm) circular needle, 40"/101.5cm long, *or size to obtain gauge*
• Stitch marker

GAUGE
32 sts and 40 rows to 4"/10cm over St st using size 1 (2.25mm) needles.
➤ Take time to check gauge.

♥ MELISSA'S TIP
KEEP PRE-SLICED VEGGIES ON HAND FOR HEART-HEALTHY SNACKS.
Eating fresh produce involves some prep time, but taking 15 minutes once or twice a week to chop up some celery sticks, broccoli florets, or cucumber spears makes grabbing a daily serving or two of veggies as easy as opening a bag of chips.

NOTE
Instructions are written using the Magic Loop method. If desired, divide sts evenly over 4 double-pointed needles.

SOCK
LEG
Cast on 60 sts. Divide into two groups of 30 sts (instep and heel), pm and join for working in the rnd. Work rows 1–24 of chart 1 once, then rep rows 1–4 of chart 2 until leg measures 7½"/19cm. Note last row of chart worked.

HEEL FLAP
Working back and forth in rows over 30 heel sts, leaving rem 30 instep sts on hold: **Row 1 (RS)** *Sl 1, k1; rep from * to end. **Row 2** Sl 1, purl to end. Rep rows 1 and 2 for 30 rows, end with a WS row.

TURN HEEL
Row 1 (RS) K17, ssk, k1, turn.
Row 2 Sl 1, p5, p2tog, p1, turn.
Row 3 Sl 1, k6, ssk, k1, turn.
Row 4 Sl 1, p7, p2tog, p1, turn.
Cont in this manner, working 1 more st before dec every row until all sts are worked—18 heel sts. Knit across heel sts, pm in center of heel to mark new beg of rnd.

GUSSET
With RS facing, pick up and k 15 sts along side of heel flap. Cont in chart 2 across 30 held instep sts. Pick up and k 15 sts along opposite side of heel flap, knit to center back of heel—78 sts.
Rnd 1 Knit to last 3 heel sts, k2tog, k1; work in pat across 30 instep sts; k1, ssk, knit to end of rnd. **Rnd 2** Work even. Rep rnds 1 and 2 until 60 sts rem.

FOOT
Work even until foot measures 8"/20.5cm or 1½"/4cm less than length of foot.

TOE
Rnd 1 Knit to last 3 heel sts, k2tog, k1; instep: k1, ssk, knit to last 3 sts, k1, k2tog; k1, ssk, knit to end of rnd. **Rnd 2** Knit. Rep rnds 1 and 2 until 16 sts rem. Graft toe using Kitchener st.

FINISHING
Weave in ends. ❤

CHART 1

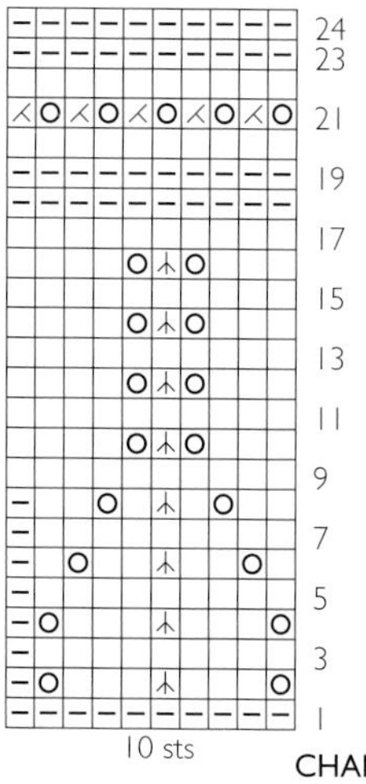

24
23
21
19
17
15
13
11
9
7
5
3
1

10 sts

CHART 2

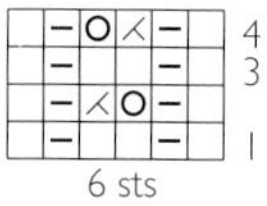

4
3
1

6 sts

STITCH KEY
☐ Knit
⊟ Purl
◩ K2tog
⋀ S2KP
◯ Yarn over

MELISSA'S STORY
Prolific knitting author and blogger Melissa Morgan-Oakes spends much of her time designing and teaching classes, but she also makes space in her schedule for daily walks with her dog, Yoshi, and eating a heart-healthy diet. In her previous job as a registered nurse, Melissa focused on educating patients and their families about many areas of health and wellness. Heart disease in particular strikes close to home for Melissa, who lost both of her grandfathers to cardiovascular disease and has several family members who have or have had heart problems. Melissa enjoys eating a wide variety of foods, including fresh fruits and veggies (especially those from local farmers), a healthy amount of lean protein, generous helpings of fiber, and a bit of healthy fats. She advocates experimenting with different fresh foods, herbs, and spices to keep your meals tasty and replace the excessive amounts of salt, sugar, and fats that make processed foods so addictive. Melissa loves kayaking in the lakes and rivers near her home in Massachusetts. And when she's short on time, she gets a good workout by doing chores on her chicken farm!

Beaded lace shawl

Knit in laceweight silk-and-cashmere yarn with a beaded edging and a subtle heart motif, this featherweight shawl is the ultimate in luxurious design.

◼◼◼▭

SIZE
Instructions are written for one size.

MEASUREMENTS
Approx 59" x 31"/150cm x 79cm

MATERIALS
• 2 2oz/55g hanks (each approx 400yd/366m) of Jade Sapphire Exotic Fibres *Silk Cashmere* (silk/cashmere) in #201 seeing red (①)
• Contrasting fingering-weight cotton (waste yarn)
• One size 4 (3.5mm) circular needle 32"/80cm long *or size to obtain gauge*
• Size 16 (.4mm) steel crochet hook or size to fit beads
• Size D/3 (3.25mm) crochet hook (for chain-st provisional cast-on)
• Stitch marker
• 1oz/30g of 8/0 Japanese seed beads in silver-lined ruby AB

GAUGES
20 sts and 40 rows to 4"/10cm over St st using size 4 (3.5mm) circular needle (before blocking). 18 sts and 36 rows to 4"/10 cm over St st using size 4 (3.5mm) circular needle (after blocking).
➤ Take time to check gauges.

NOTES
1) Shawl is knit from top down.
2) Charts show RS rows only.
3) Chart 1 is worked once on either side of center st. Charts 2 and 3 are worked once across row.
4) Beads are added with crochet hook.

STITCH GLOSSARY
Add Bead Slip bead onto shank of crochet hook. With hook facing you, slip next st from LH needle onto crochet hook. Hold taut. Slip bead onto st. Slip st back to LH needle and knit.

SHAWL
With crochet hook and waste yarn, ch 8 for chain-st provisional cast-on. Cut yarn and draw end though lp on hook. Turn ch so bottom lps are at top and cut end is at left. With circular needle, beg 2 lps from right end, pick up and k 1 st in each of next 3 lps— 3 sts. Work 7 rows in garter st (knit every row).

Next row Pick up and purl 3 sts along side edge; release cut end from lp of waste yarn ch, then pulling out 1 ch at a time, place 3 live sts onto LH needle, then k these 3 sts—9 sts.

BEG CHART 1
Row 1 (RS) K4, yo for chart row 1, place marker, k1 for center st, yo for chart row, k4—11 sts.
Row 2 and all WS rows K3, p to last 3 sts, slipping marker, k3.
Row 3 K4, work chart row 3, sl marker, k1 for center st, work chart row 3, k4. Cont to work chart in this manner through row 50—107 sts.
Row 51 (2nd line of numbers) K4, *work chart row 31 to 10-st rep, work 10-st rep 3 times, work to end of chart row*, k1, rep from * to *, k4. Cont to work chart 1 in this manner through row 70—147 sts.

BEG CHART 2
Row 71 (RS) K4, work chart 2 row, k4.
Rows 72 and all WS rows K3, p to last 3 sts, slipping marker, k3. Cont to work chart 2 in this manner through row 90—187 sts.

WORK CHART 1
Row 91 (3rd line of numbers) K4, *work chart row to 10-st rep, work 10-st rep 7 times, work to end of chart row *, k1, rep from

ANDREA'S STORY
Andrea has an amazing talent for creating exquisite and inspired lace designs. She also happens to be a nurse practitioner, and we are so happy to include her experience as a health care professional, as well as one of her gorgeous designs, in *Knit Red*. One of Andrea's earliest areas of interest was pediatric cardiology, and she points out that while heart disease is often thought of as something that affects only older adults, in reality it can be found in every age group. After working with infants and children struggling with serious heart disease, Andrea encourages everyone, young and old, to eat a healthy diet and make time in your schedule for some daily exercise—it is never too early or too late to be healthy! Andrea and her family keep their diet lean and mean (and delicious!) by dining on fresh local foods as often as possible, rarely eating meat, and choosing whole grains over processed wheat products. They also like to wind down after dinner with a glass of red wine and some dark chocolate—yum!

* to *, k4. Cont to work chart 1 in this manner through row 110—227 sts.

WORK CHART 2
Row 111 (2nd line of numbers) K4, work chart row to 20-st rep, work 20-st rep 4 times, work to next 20-st rep line, work 20-st rep 4 times, work to end of chart, k4. Cont to work chart 2

in this manner through row 130—267 sts.

WORK CHART 1
Row 131 (4th line of numbers) K4, *work chart row to 10-st rep, work 10-st rep 11 times, work to end of chart row*, k1, rep from * to *, k4. Cont to work chart 1 in this manner through row 149—307 sts.

BORDER
BEG CHART 3
(Note The 20-st rep in chart 3 is mirrored on the right and left sides of center st.)
Row 1 (RS) K4, work chart row to 20-st rep, work 20-st rep 7 times, work chart row to next 20-st rep, work 20-st rep 7 times, work to end of row.
Row 2 and all WS rows through row 20 K3, p to last 3 sts, slipping marker, k3. Cont to work chart 3 in this manner until row 21 is complete.
Row 22 (WS) Knit.

BEG SHORT ROWS
(Note Short rows are worked across row 23 to shape the scalloped border.)

SCALLOP 1
Work short row sequence as foll: **(RS)** K10, yo, k1, turn. **(WS)** K3, yo, k1, turn. K5, yo, k1, turn. K7, yo, k1, turn. Cont in this manner, working 2 more sts before yo every row until k15, yo, k1, has been worked. Turn, k18.

SCALLOPS 2–8
[Work short row sequence as for scallop 1 until k35, yo, k1, has been worked. Turn, k38] 7 times.

SCALLOPS 9 AND 10
(Note These scallops are worked on either side of the center stitch) [Work short row sequence as for scallop 1 until k35, yo, k1 has been worked. Turn, k39] twice.

SCALLOPS 11–17
Work same as for scallops 2–8.

SCALLOP 18
K5, yo, k1, turn. K3, yo, k1, turn. K5, yo, k1, turn. K7, yo, k1, turn. Cont to work short rows, working 2 more sts into scallop until k15, yo, k1, has been worked. Turn, k22. There are 650 sts.
Row (inc) 24 (WS) K4, M1, k to center st, M1, remove marker, k center st, M1, k to last 4 sts, M1, k4—654 sts. Bind off as foll: *K2tog, add bead to resulting st and sl st back to LH needle; rep from * until all sts have been worked. Fasten off.

FINISHING
To block, wet shawl thoroughly. Lay flat and pin to measurements, shaping scallops while pinning. Sample was blocked using blocking wires along the straight upper edge. Let dry completely before removing wires and unpinning.❤

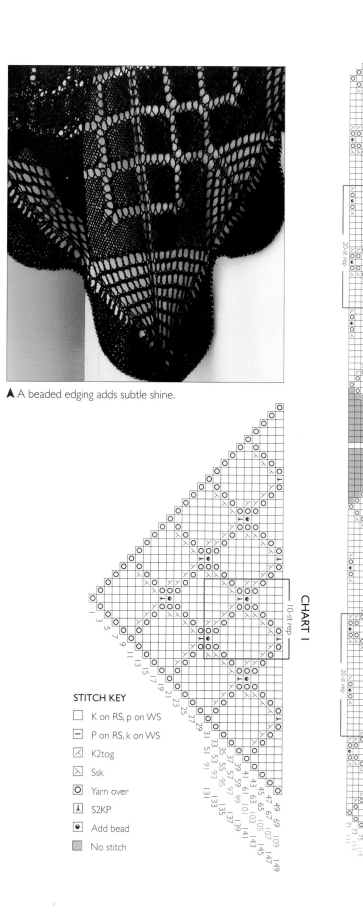

▲ A beaded edging adds subtle shine.

STITCH KEY

☐ K on RS, p on WS

⊟ P on RS, k on WS

⊠ K2tog

⊠ Ssk

⊙ Yarn over

⅄ S2KP

⦿ Add bead

▨ No stitch

CHART I

10-st rep

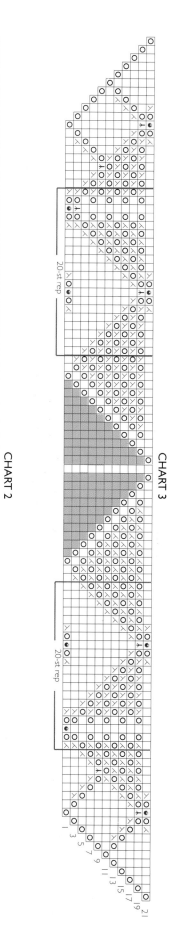

CHART 2

20-st rep

CHART 3

20-st rep

Reversible wristers

Kit and her design team at Churchmouse Yarns & Teas love simple projects that are easy to knit and can be worn different ways. These versatile handwarmers can morph into a number of fetching configurations.

◖■■■▢

SIZE
Instructions are written for one size.

MEASUREMENTS
HAND CIRCUMFERENCE (unstretched) 7½"/19cm
LENGTH 8½"/21.5cm

MATERIALS
• 1.88oz/25g hank (approx 330yd/300m) of Shibui *Silk Cloud* (kid mohair/silk) each in #430 cranberry (MC) and #2013 peony (CC) (❶)
• Contrasting size 10 crochet thread (waste yarn)
• One set (4) size 1 (2.25mm) double-pointed needles (dpns) *or size to obtain gauge*
• Three spare size 1 (2.25mm) double-pointed needles (dpns)
• Size D/3 (3.25mm) crochet hook (for chain-st provisional cast-on)
• Stitch marker

GAUGE
30 sts and 52 rnds to 4"/10cm over St st using size 1 (2.25mm) dpns.
➤ Take time to check gauge.

WRISTERS
With crochet hook and waste yarn, ch 62 for chain-st provisional cast-on. Cut yarn and draw end though lp on hook; do not pull too tightly. Turn ch so bottom lps are at top and cut end is at left. With CC and dpns, beg 2 lps from right end, then pick up and k 1 st in each of next 57 lps—57 sts. Divide sts evenly over 3 needles (19 sts on each). Join, taking care not to twist sts on needles, pm for beg of rnds. Cont in St st (knit every rnd) until piece measures 8½"/21.5cm from beg. Change to MC and cont to work in St st for 8½"/21.5cm. Cut MC, leaving a 2yd/2m tail for sewing.

FINISHING
Bring provisional cast-on edge to inside of wrister, so CC is on inside and WS of CC and MC are facing. Release cut end from lp of waste yarn ch. Pulling out 1 ch at a time, place 57 live CC sts onto 3 dpns (19 sts on each). Using MC tail, graft MC to CC using Kitchener stitch.

I-CORDS (MAKE 2)
With dpns and MC, cast on 4 sts, leaving a long tail for sewing. Work in I-cord as foll:
*Next row (RS) With 2nd dpn, k4, do not turn. Slide sts back to beg of needle to work next row from RS; rep from * for 20"/51cm. Cut yarn, leaving a 6"/15cm tail, and thread through rem sts. Pull tog tightly, then secure and weave in end. Thread beg tail in tapestry needle, then sew running stitches around top (cast-on) edge. Pull tog tightly to close opening, then secure and weave in end.

SHIRRING
Shift layers of each wrister so desired amount of CC (or MC) is showing, then determine top and bottom edges. Thread one end of I-cord into a large-eye yarn needle. With RS facing, beg 2½"/6.5cm from bottom edge. Working between 2 sts and both layers, weave tie under 6 rows and over 6 rows for approx 4"/10cm, ending on WS and 2"/5cm from top edge. Bring needle up to RS, 2 sts from opposite gathering row. Weave back to the beg, foll same weaving pat, ending on RS. Even up ends, draw cord up to gather, then tie ends in a bow. ❤

KIT'S STORY
A few of us at Jimmy Beans have had the distinct pleasure of visiting Kit's charming shop, Churchmouse Yarns & Teas on Bainbridge Island (a short ferry ride from Seattle, Washington). When we approached Kit about contributing to *Knit Red*, she was stunned to hear the devastating statistics regarding heart disease in women and immediately pledged her support. Kit was prompted to reevaluate some of her less healthy habits, but that isn't to say she didn't have some great heart-healthy routines already in place. She and her husband, John, enjoy a warm bowl of oatmeal every morning along with a cup of tea, a great source of antioxidants. She also takes advantage of the local produce from small Bainbridge Island farms, and living on an island in the Pacific Northwest ensures the year-round availability of fresh salmon. As for staying active, Kit often finds she lacks motivation to swap her knitting needles for walking shoes, so she takes it with her. Her favorite form of exercise is going for a walk on the golf course with John. While he golfs, she knits—they've dubbed it "knolfing"!

Omit the I-cord lacings and turn the mitts partly or completely inside out for different color effects.

Cabled cardi

You'll feel like the queen of hearts in this romantic cardigan with its exquisite details, including a sweetheart neckline, abbreviated button band, and a cables-and-knots stitch pattern.

■■■□

SIZES
Instructions are written for size Small. Changes for Medium and Large are in parentheses. (Shown in size Small.)

MEASUREMENTS
BUST 35 (39, 43)"/89 (99, 109)cm
LENGTH 22½ (23½, 24½)"/57 (59.5, 62)cm
UPPER ARM 12½ (13½, 14½)"/32 (34.5, 37)cm

MATERIALS
• 6 (6, 7) 3½oz/100g balls (each approx 217yd/198m) of Berroco *Vintage* (acrylic/wool/nylon) in #5150 berries **(4)**
• One pair size 7 (4.5mm) needles *or size to obtain gauge*
• Size 5 (3.75mm) circular needle, 24"/60cm long
• Stitch holders
• Three ⅞"/22mm buttons

GAUGES
20 sts and 27 rows to 4"/10cm over St st using larger needles.
21 sts and 27 rows to 4"/10cm over moss st using larger needles.
➤ Take time to check gauges.

STITCH GLOSSARY
2-st RC Sl 1 st to cn and hold to *back*, k1, k1 from cn.
2-st LC Sl 1 st to cn and hold to *front*, k1, k1 from cn.
4-st RC Sl 2 sts to cn and hold to *back*, k2, k2 from cn.
4-st LC Sl 2 sts to cn and hold to *front*, k2, k2 from cn.

MOSS STITCH
(over an even number of sts)
Rows 1 (RS) and 2 *K1, p1;
rep from * to end.
Rows 3 and 4 *P1, k1;
rep from * to end.
Rep rows 1–4 for moss st.

K2, P2 RIB
(over multiple of 4 sts plus 2)
Row 1 (WS) P2, *k2, p2;
rep from * to end.
Row 2 K2, *p2, k2;
rep from * to end.
Rep rows 1 and 2 for pat.

NORAH'S STORY
Norah Gaughan's unique yet timeless designs never cease to captivate us. She grew up in a creative household, learning to crochet from her mother and grandmother at a young age. Norah studied both biology and studio art in college and combines her backgrounds to create knits inspired by patterns found in nature, such as spirals, pentagons, fractals, and waves. As the design director at Berroco yarns, Norah is very involved in the knitting community, and she jumped at the chance to promote heart health for women, knitters, and their friends and families. As longtime fans of Norah's work, we were elated when she agreed to contribute to *Knit Red!*

❤ NORAH'S TIPS
NORAH LIKES TO TAKE THE STAIRS IN LIEU OF THE ELEVATOR whenever she can, especially on the way up! Unless you've got twenty flights to climb, walking usually takes about the same amount of time as riding, and it gives your heart, and legs, a nice mini-workout.

MAKE KNOT

K into the front, back, and front of one st, slip back to LH needle, k3, sl 2nd and first sts over 3rd st.

CARDIGAN

BACK

With smaller needles, cast on 102 (110, 122) sts. Work in k2, p2 rib for 2½"/6.5cm, end with a RS row. Change to larger needles.

Next row (WS) Purl, dec 10 (8, 10) sts evenly across—92 (102, 112) sts. Work in moss st for 1"/2.5cm, ending with a WS row.

WAIST SHAPING

Next (dec) row (RS) K1, k2tog, work to last 3 sts, ssk, k1—2 sts dec. Rep dec row every 6th row 3 times—84 (94, 104) sts. Work even until piece measures 10"/25.5cm from beg, ending with a WS row.

Next (inc) row (RS) K1, M1, work to last st, M1, k1—2 sts inc. Rep inc row every 6th row 3 times—92 (102, 112) sts. Work even until piece measures 11½ (12, 12½)"/29 (30.5, 32)cm from beg, ending with a WS row.

ARMHOLE SHAPING

Bind off 3 (4, 6) sts at beg of next 2 rows. Bind off 2 sts at beg of next 4 rows.

Next (dec) row (RS) K1, k2tog, work to last 3 sts, ssk, k1—2 sts dec. Rep dec row every other row 2 (4, 5) times—72 (76, 80) sts. Work even until armholes measure 7½ (8, 8½)"/19 (20.5, 21.5)cm, ending with a WS row.

NECK AND SHOULDER SHAPING

Bind off 7 (7, 9) sts at beg of next 2 rows. Bind off 7 (8, 8) sts at beg of next 4 rows. Bind off rem 30 sts for back neck.

RIGHT FRONT

With smaller needles, cast on 55 (59, 63) sts.

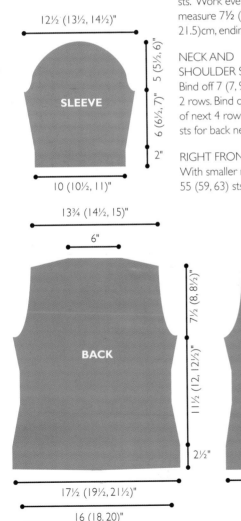

12½ (13½, 14½)"

5 (5½, 6)"

SLEEVE

6 (6½, 7)"

2"

10 (10½, 11)"

13¾ (14½, 15)"

6"

BACK

7½ (8, 8½)"

11½ (12, 12½)"

2½"

17½ (19½, 21½)"

16 (18, 20)"

Row 1 (WS) P2, *k2, p2; rep from * to last 5 sts, k2, p3.

Row 2 Sl 3 purlwise, p2, *k2, p2; rep from *, end k2.

Rep rows 1 and 2 for 2½"/6.5cm, ending with a RS row. Change to larger needles.

Next row (WS) Purl, dec 2 (2, 0) sts evenly spaced to last 5 sts, k2, p3—53 (57, 63) sts.

Next row Sl 3 purlwise, p2, work chart over next 30 sts, work moss st to end. Work even as established for 1"/2.5cm, ending with a WS row.

WAIST SHAPING

Next (dec) row (RS) Work to last 3 sts, ssk, k1—1 st dec. Rep dec row every 6th row 3 times—49 (53, 59) sts. Work even until piece measures 10"/25.5cm from beg, ending with a WS row.

Next (inc) row (RS) Work to last st, M1, k1—1 st inc. Rep inc row every 6th row 3 times—53 (57, 63) sts. Work even until piece measures 14 (14½, 15)"/35.5 (37, 38)cm, ending with a WS row.

NECK AND ARMHOLE SHAPING

Row 1 (RS) Slip the first three sts tog (neck edge), p1, psso, bind off 2 more sts, work to end.

Row 2 Bind off 3 (4, 6) sts (armhole edge), work to end. Cont in pat, binding off 3 sts at neck edge twice and binding off 2 sts at armhole edge 4 times—31 (34, 38) sts. Dec 1 st at neck edge every other row 3 times, and at the same time dec 1 st at armhole edge every other row 3 (5, 6) times—25 (26, 29) sts. Work even for 1"/2.5cm, end with a WS row.

Next (inc) row (RS) K1, M1, work in pat to end. Rep inc row every 4th (2nd, 4th) row 7 (8, 7) times—33 (35, 37) sts. At the same time, shape shoulders when piece measures same as back to shoulders.

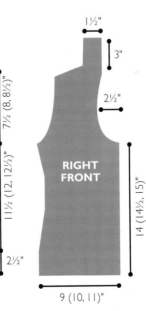

1½"

3"

2½"

RIGHT FRONT

14 (14½, 15)"

9 (10, 11)"

SHOULDER SHAPING

Bind off 7 (7, 9) sts at beg of next WS row. Bind off 7 (8, 8) sts at beg of next 2 WS rows—12 sts rem for back collar. Work even for 3"/7.5cm. Place on holder and cut yarn, leaving a long tail.

LEFT FRONT

With smaller needles, cast on 55 (59, 63) sts.

Row 1 (WS) Sl 3 purlwise, k2, *p2, k2; rep from *, ending p2.

Row 2 K2, *p2, k2; rep from * to last 5 sts, p2, k3.

Rep rows 1 and 2 for 2½"/6.5cm, ending with a RS row. Change to larger needles.

Next row (WS) Sl 3 purlwise, k2, purl to end, dec 2 (2, 0) sts evenly spaced—53 (57, 63) sts.

Next row Work in moss st to last 35 sts, work row 1 of chart over next 30 sts, p2, k3. Work even in pat for 1"/2.5cm, ending with a WS row.

WAIST SHAPING

Next (dec) row (RS) K1, k2tog, work to end—1 st dec. Rep dec row every 6th row 3 times—49 (53, 59) sts. Work even until piece measures 10"/25.5cm from beg, end with a WS row.

Next (inc) row (RS) K1, M1, work to end—1 st inc. Rep inc row every 6th row 3 times—53 (57, 63) sts. Work even until piece measures 14 (14½, 15)"/35.5 (37, 38)cm, end with a RS row.

NECK AND ARMHOLE SHAPING

Row 1 (WS) Slip the first three sts tog (neck edge), p1, psso, bind off 2 more sts, work in pat to end.

Row 2 Bind off 3 (4, 6) sts (armhole edge), work in pat to end. Cont in pat, binding off 3 sts at neck edge twice and binding off 2 sts at armhole edge 4 times—31 (34, 38) sts. Dec 1 st at neck edge every other row 3

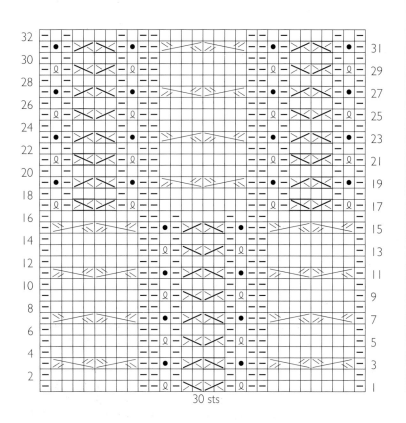

STITCH KEY

☐ K on RS, p on WS	⧯ 2-st RC
⊟ P on RS, k on WS	⧯ 2-st LC
● Make knot	⧯ 4-st RC
ℚ K1 tbl	⧯ 4-st LC

30 sts

times, and at the same time dec 1 st at armhole edge every other row 3 (5, 6) times—25 (26, 29) sts. Work even for 1"/2.5cm, ending with a WS row.
Next (inc) row (RS) Work to last st, M1, k1. Rep inc row every 4th (2nd, 4th) row 7 (8, 7) times—33 (35, 37) sts. At the same time, shape shoulders when piece measures same as back to shoulders.

SHOULDER SHAPING
Bind off 7 (7, 9) sts at beg of next RS row. Bind off 7 (8, 8) sts at beg of next 2 RS rows—12 sts rem for back collar. Work even for 3"/7.5cm. Place on holder and cut yarn, leaving a long tail.

SLEEVES
With smaller needles, cast on 54 (54, 58) sts. Work in k2, p2 rib for 2"/5cm, ending with a RS row. Change to larger needles. Purl 1 row, inc 0 (2, 0) sts evenly spaced. Work in moss st for 1"/2.5cm, ending with a WS row.
Next (inc) row (RS) K1, M1, work to last st, M1, k1—2 sts inc. Rep inc row every 6th (6th, 4th) row 5 (6, 8) times—66 (70, 76) sts. Work even in pat until piece measures 8 (8½, 9)"/ 20.5 (21.5, 23)cm, ending with a WS row.

CAP SHAPING
Bind off 3 (4, 6) sts at beg of next 2 rows. Bind off 2 sts at beg of next 2 rows—56 (58, 60) sts.
Next (dec) row (RS) K1, k2tog, work to last 3 sts, ssk, k1—2 sts

dec. Rep dec row every other row 11 (12, 13) times. Work 0 (2, 4) rows even. Bind off 2 sts at beg of next 2 rows. Bind off 3 sts at beg of next 2 rows. Bind off rem 22 sts.

FINISHING
Sew shoulder seams. Set in sleeves. Sew side and sleeve seams. Join ends of collar (sts on holders) using Kitchener st, then sew side edge to back neck.

FRONT BANDS
Mark 5½"/14cm down from front neck on each side.

LEFT FRONT BAND
With RS facing and smaller needles, pick up and k 34 sts from neck edge to marker.

Work in k2, p2 rib for 1"/2.5cm. Bind off.

RIGHT FRONT BAND
With RS facing and smaller needles, pick up and k 34 sts from marker
to neck edge. Work in k2, p2 rib for 1 row.
Next row (RS) Work 3 sts in pat, bind off 2 sts, *work in pat until 11 sts after bind-off, bind off 2 sts; rep from * once more, work to end.
Next row Cast on 2 sts over bound-off sts for buttonholes. Cont in rib until band measures 1"/2.5cm. Bind off.

Block pieces to measurements. Weave in ends. Sew buttons opposite buttonholes. ❤

Dolman sleeve sweater

A jaunty white bow enlivens this solid red sweater. The fitted waist and three-quarter-length sleeves give it a modern feel.

▪▪▪▪▶

SIZES

Instructions are written for size X-Small. Changes for Small, Medium, Large, X-Large, XX-Large, and XXX-Large are in parentheses. (Shown in size X-Small.)

MEASUREMENTS

BUST 36 (39½, 41, 44, 46½, 49, 51½)"/91.5 (100, 104, 111.5, 118, 124.5, 131)cm

LENGTH 20¾ (21¼, 21½, 22, 22¼, 22¾, 23)"/52.5 (54, 54.5, 56, 56.5, 58, 58.5)cm

UPPER ARM 16½ (17½, 17½, 18, 18½, 19, 19½)"/42 (44.5, 44.5, 45.5, 47, 48, 49.5)cm

MATERIALS

• 9 (9, 10, 10, 11, 11, 12) 1¾oz/50g balls (each approx 137yd/125m) of Debbie Bliss *Baby Cashmerino* (merino wool/microfiber/cashmere) in #34 red (MC) **2**

• 1 ball in #100 white (CC)

• One pair each sizes 1, 2, and 3 (2.25, 2.75, and 3.25mm) needles *or size to obtain gauge*

• Three size 3 (3.25mm) circular needles, 29"/75cm long

• One size 2 (2.75mm) circular needle, 16"/40cm long

• Stitch holders

• Stitch marker

GAUGE

25 sts and 34 rows to 4"/10cm over St st using size 3 (3.25mm) needles.
▶ Take time to check gauge.

SHORT ROW WRAP & TURN (W&T) ON RS ROW (ON WS ROW)

1) Wyib (wyif), sl next st purlwise.
2) Move yarn between the needles to the front (back).
3) Sl the same st back to LH needle. Turn work. One st is wrapped.
4) When working the wrapped st, insert RH needle under the wrap and work it tog with the corresponding st on needle.

K1, P1 RIB

(over a multiple of 2 sts plus 1)

Row 1 (RS) K1, *p1, k1; rep from * to end.
Row 2 P1, *k1, p1; rep from * to end.
Rep rows 1 and 2 for k1, p1 rib.

BACK

With size 2 needles and MC, cast on 99 (107, 115, 123, 131, 139, 147) sts. Work in k1, p1 rib for 4¾"/12cm, ending with a WS row. Change to size 3 needles. Cont in St st (k on RS and p on WS) and work even for 2 rows.

SIDE SHAPING

Inc row (RS) K3, M1, knit to last 3 sts, M1, k3—101 (109, 117, 125, 133, 141, 149) sts. Rep inc row every 6th row 6 times more—113 (121, 129, 137, 145, 153, 161) sts. Work even until piece measures 11¾ (11¾, 12¼, 12¼, 12½, 12½, 13)"/30 (30, 31, 31, 32, 32, 33)cm from beg, end with a WS row. Change to larger circular needle.

SLEEVE SHAPING

Cast on 8 sts at beg of next 4 rows, 10 sts at beg of next 6 rows, then 12 sts at beg of next 4 rows—253 (261, 269, 277, 285, 293, 301) sts. Work even until piece measures 18½ (19, 19¼, 19¾, 20, 20½, 20¾)"/47 (48, 49, 50, 51, 52, 53)cm from beg, ending with a WS row.

UPPER SLEEVE AND SHOULDER SHAPING

Note Short rows are not symmetrical.
Next 2 rows Knit to last 10 sts,

DEBBIE'S STORY

We were delighted when iconic knitwear designer Debbie Bliss joined our campaign to spread awareness of heart disease. Debbie's experiences with the disease speak both to its destructive nature and to our ability to take steps to prevent it. Debbie's maternal grandfather died of heart disease at the age of 32, and she has lost all of her uncles to heart disease. This family history encourages Debbie to get regular check-ups. Strangely enough, her regular EKGs indicate heart disease, but all other tests show her to be completely heart healthy, something for which she is extremely grateful. To keep her heart healthy and disease-free Debbie takes her dogs for a 20-minute walk every day, which is good for their hearts, too!

♥ **DEBBIE'S TIP**

A SELF-PROCLAIMED LOVER OF GREASY FOOD, Debbie considers it a huge achievement that she is able to avoid eating artery-clogging meals on a daily basis. She recommends rewarding yourself with a favorite unhealthy meal once a month as a treat for eating healthy the rest of the time!

sl 1, w&t; purl to last 11 sts, sl 1, w&t.
Next 2 rows Knit to last 21 sts, sl 1, w&t; purl to last 22 sts, sl 1, w&t.
Next 2 rows Knit to last 32 sts, sl 1, w&t; purl to last 33 sts, sl 1, w&t.
Next 2 rows Knit to last 43 sts, sl 1, w&t; purl to last 44 sts, sl 1, w&t.
Next 2 rows Knit to last 54 sts, sl 1, w&t; purl to last 55 sts, sl 1, w&t.
Next 2 rows Knit to last 65 sts, sl 1, w&t; purl to last 66 sts, sl 1, w&t.
Next 2 rows Knit to last 76 sts, sl 1, w&t; purl to last 77 sts, sl 1, w&t.
Next 2 rows Knit to last 86 (87, 88, 89, 90, 91, 92) sts, sl 1, w&t; purl to last 87 (88, 89, 90, 91, 92, 93) sts, sl 1, w&t.
Next 2 rows Knit to last 96 (98, 100, 102, 104, 106, 108) sts, sl 1, w&t; purl to last 97 (99, 101, 103, 105, 107, 109) sts, sl 1, w&t.
Next 2 rows Knit to last 106 (109, 112, 115, 118, 121, 124) sts, sl 1, w&t; purl to last 107 (110, 113, 116, 119, 122, 125) sts, sl 1, w&t.

FRONT

Work as for back to upper sleeve and shoulder shaping—253 (261, 269, 277, 285, 293, 301) sts.

UPPER SLEEVE AND SHOULDER SHAPING

Note Short rows are not symmetrical.
Next row (RS) K 119 (122, 125, 128, 131, 134, 137), turn and cont on these sts for first side of front neck.
Next row Bind off 2 sts, purl to last 16 sts, sl 1, w&t—117 sts.
Next row Knit to end.
Next row Bind off 2 sts, purl to last 27 sts, sl 1, w&t—115 sts.
Next row Knit to end.
Next row Bind off 2 sts, purl to last 38 sts, sl 1, w&t—113 sts.
Next row Knit to end.
Next row Bind off 2 sts, purl to last 49 sts, sl 1, w&t—111 sts.
Next row Knit to end.
Next row Bind off 2 sts, purl to last 60 sts, sl 1, w&t—109 sts.
Next row Knit to end.
Next row Bind off 2 sts, purl to last 71 sts, sl 1, w&t—107 sts.
Next row Knit to end.
Next row Purl to last 82sts, sl 1, w&t.
Next row Knit to end.
Next row Purl to last 93 (94, 95, 96, 97, 98, 99) sts, sl 1, w&t.
Next row Knit to end.
Next row Purl to last 103 (105, 107, 109, 111, 113, 115) sts, sl 1, w&t.
Next row Knit to end.
Next row P4, sl 1, w&t.
Next row Knit to end. Place rem 107 (110, 113, 116, 119, 122, 125) sts on spare circular needle. With RS facing, place center 15 (17, 19, 21, 23, 25, 27) sts on holder for front neck.
Next row (RS) Rejoin yarn to rem sts, knit to end.
Next row Purl to end.
Next row Bind off 2 sts, knit to last 26 sts, sl 1, w&t—117 sts.
Next row Purl to end.
Next row Bind off 2 sts, knit to last 37 sts, sl 1, w&t—115 sts.
Next row Purl to end.
Next row Bind off 2 sts, knit to last 48 sts, sl 1, w&t—113 sts.
Next row Purl to end.
Next row Bind off 2 sts, knit to last 59 sts, sl 1, w&t—111 sts.
Next row Purl to end.
Next row Bind off 2 sts, knit to last 70 sts, sl 1, w&t—109 sts.
Next row Purl to end.
Next row Bind off 2 sts, knit to last 81 sts, sl 1, w&t—107 sts.
Next row Purl to end.
Next row Knit to last 92 (93, 94, 95, 96, 97, 98) sts, sl 1, w&t.
Next row Purl to end.
Next row Knit to last 103 (105, 107, 109, 111, 113, 115) sts, sl 1, w&t.
Next row Purl to end.
Next row K3, sl 1, w&t.
Next row Purl to end. Leave rem 107 (110, 113, 116, 119, 122, 125) sts on needle.

BOW

With size 1 needles and CC, cast on 25 sts. Work in garter st (knit every row) for 5"/12.5cm.
Bind off knitwise.

LOOP

With size 1 needles and MC, cast on 6 sts. Work in garter st for 2"/5cm. Bind off knitwise.

FINISHING

Block pieces lightly to measurements. With WS tog, join upper sleeve and shoulder each side using 3-needle bind-off, placing center 39 (41, 43, 45, 47, 49, 51) sts on holder for back neck.

NECK BAND

With RS facing, size 2 (2.75mm) circular needle, and MC, beg at left shoulder seam and pick up and k 24 sts evenly along left front neck edge, k 15 (17, 19, 21, 23, 25, 27) sts from front neck holder, pick up and k 24 sts evenly spaced along right neck edge, then k 39 (41, 43, 45, 47, 49, 51) sts from back neck holder—102 (106, 110, 114, 118, 122, 126) sts. Join and pm for beg of rnds. Work in k1, p1 rib for 7 rnds. Bind off loosely in rib.

CUFFS

With RS facing, size 2 (2.75mm) needles, and MC, pick up and k 65 (69, 73, 77, 77, 81, 81) sts evenly spaced along sleeve edge. Beg with row 2, cont in k1, p1 rib for 2"/5cm, end with a WS row. Bind off on rib. Sew side and sleeve seams.

BOW

Sew short edges of bow loop tog. Insert bow through loop, then center side to side. Using MC, sew bow to loop. Referring to photo, pin bow to upper right front bodice of sweater, then sew in place using MC.❤

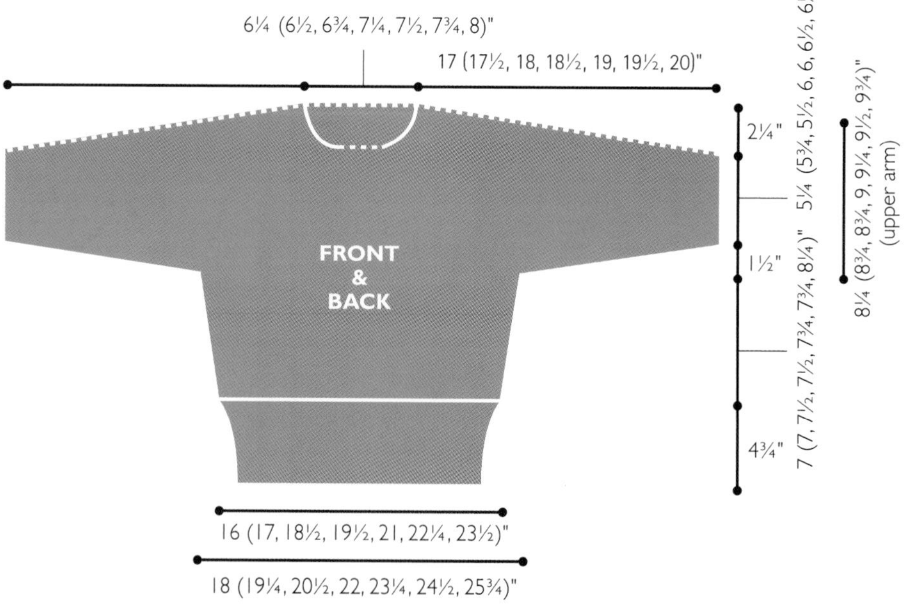
6¼ (6½, 6¾, 7¼, 7½, 7¾, 8)"
17 (17½, 18, 18½, 19, 19½, 20)"
2¼"
1½"
4¾"
5¼ (5¾, 5½, 6, 6, 6½, 6¼)"
7 (7, 7½, 7½, 7¾, 7¾, 8¼)"
8¼ (8¾, 8¾, 9, 9¼, 9½, 9¾)"
(upper arm)
FRONT
&
BACK
16 (17, 18½, 19½, 21, 22¼, 23½)"
18 (19¼, 20½, 22, 23¼, 24½, 25¾)"

● DEBORAH NEWTON

Leaf lace sweater

This warm and cozy cardigan is a veritable stitch sampler, in which seed stitch, stockinette stitch, twisted cables, and eyelet panels gracefully merge into a lovely leaf lace border.

SIZES

Instructions are written for size Small. Changes for Medium and Large are in parentheses. (Shown in size Small.)

MEASUREMENTS

BUST 38 (41, 44)"/96.5 (104, 111.5)cm
LENGTH 25 (26½, 28)"/63.5 (67, 71)cm
UPPER ARM 14 (15, 15¾)"/35.5 (38, 40)cm

MATERIALS

• 13 (14, 16) 1¾ oz/50g balls (each approx 131yd/120m) of SMC Select *Silk Wool* (wool/silk/polyamide) in #7101 red ⑤
• One pair size 9 (5.5mm) needles *or size to obtain gauge*
• One pair size 8 (5mm) needles
• Cable needle
• Stitch markers
• Stitch holders or waste yarn
• Six 1⅛"/29mm buttons

GAUGES

18 sts and 26 rows to 4"/10cm over St st using larger needles.
19 sts and 26 rows to 4"/10cm over pat using larger needles.
➤ Take time to check gauges.

STITCH GLOSSARY

RT (right twist) K2tog but do not slip from needle; insert needle between sts just knit and knit the first st again; slip both sts from needle.

LEAF BORDER

(over 23 sts)
Row 1 (RS) K8, k2tog, yo, k1, p1, k1, yo, ssk, k8.
Row 2 P7, p2tog tbl, p2, yo, k1, yo, p2, p2tog, p7.
Row 3 K6, k2tog, k1, yo, k2, p1, k2, yo, k1, ssk, k6.
Row 4 P5, p2tog tbl, p3, yo, p1, k1, p1, yo, p3, p2tog, p5.
Row 5 K4, k2tog, k2, yo, k3, p1, k3, yo, k2, ssk, k4.
Row 6 P3, p2tog tbl, p4, yo, p2, k1, p2, yo, p4, p2tog, p3.
Row 7 K2, k2tog, k3, yo, k4, p1, k4, yo, k3, ssk, k2.
Row 8 P1, p2tog tbl, p5, yo, p3, k1, p3, yo, p5, p2tog, p1.
Row 9 K2tog, k4, yo, k5, p1, k5, yo, k4, ssk.
Row 10 P11, k1, p11.
Row 11 K11, p1, k11.
Row 12 P11, k1, p11.

TWIST CABLE

(over 10 sts)
Row 1 (RS) P2, [RT] 3 times, p2.
Row 2 K2, p6, k2.
Row 3 P2, k1, [RT] twice, k1, p2.
Row 4 K2, p6, k2.
Rep rows 1–4 for pat.

SEED STITCH

(over an odd number of sts)
Row 1 (WS) K1, *p1, k1; rep from * to end. Rep row 1 for pat.

EYELET PANEL

(over 7 sts)
Row 1 (WS) K2, p3, k2.
Row 2 P2, k2tog, yo, k1, p2.
Row 3 Rep row 1.
Row 4 P2, k1, yo, ssk, p2.
Rep rows 1–4 for pat.

K1, P1 RIB

(over an odd number of sts)
Row 1 (WS) K1, *p1, k1; rep from * to end.
Row 2 P1, *k1, p1; rep from * to end.
Rep rows 1–2 for pat.

NOTE

Work sleeves first to learn the patterns and their placement, so the shaping decreases can be worked in body pieces with greater ease.

SLEEVES

With larger needles, cast on 80 (84, 88) sts. Purl 1 row.
Next row (RS) K2 (4, 6) (St st edge sts), pm, work row 1 of twist cable over 10 sts, pm, work row 1 of leaf border over 23 sts, pm, work row 1 of twist cable over center 10 sts, pm, work row 1 of leaf border over 23 sts, pm, work row 1 of twist cable over 10 sts, pm, k2 (4, 6) (St st edge sts).
Working in pats as established, work even until 4 reps of leaf border pat are complete, 48 rows total, end with a WS row. Piece measures approx 7 ½"/19cm.

CHANGE PATTERNS

Next row (RS) K2 (4, 6) (edge sts), slip marker, cable over 10 sts, slip marker, k10, S2KP, k10 (now 21 sts in this section), slip marker, cable over 10 sts, slip marker, k10, S2KP, k10 (now 21 sts in this

DEBORAH'S STORY
Deborah Newton is a prolific knitwear designer and best-selling author who has been creating stunning garments for more than 30 years. She keeps her energy up and her heart fit with daily exercise. She tries to walk twice a day, one of those times with her cocker spaniel, Brownie, and has been a practitioner of Iyengar yoga for many years. The experiences of several family members with heart disease have made Deborah acutely aware of the importance of diet and exercise. Her mother had scarlet fever as a child, which damaged the mitral valve of her heart and eventually led to a valve replacement. One of her uncles died after suffering a heart attack as a young man, and her beloved father-in-law was diagnosed with heart disease before he passed away. Deborah believes that awareness and education are the key to combating this deadly disease.

● **DEBORAH'S TIP**
WHEN MEETING UP WITH FRIENDS, skip the coffee shop and take a walk! A brisk stroll around the park or a ramble through the hills is a great way to catch up while sharing the benefits of exercise.

CAP SHAPING
Bind off 5 (6, 7) sts at beg of next 2 rows—57 (59, 61) sts.
Next (dec) row (RS) K1, ssk, work to the last 3 sts, end k2tog, k1—55 (57, 59) sts.
Next row P2 (4, 6), work as established to last 2 (4, 6) sts, end p2 (4, 6).
Rep the last 2 rows 15 (17, 20) times—25 (23, 19) sts.
Next row (RS) Bind off 9 (8, 6) sts, work to the last 3 sts, end k2tog, k1.
Next row Work even.
Rep the last 2 rows once more, then bind off rem 5 sts on last RS row.

LEFT FRONT
LOWER BORDER
With larger needles, cast on 80 (84, 88) sts. Purl 1 row. Work as for lower sleeve for 48 rows.

CHANGE PATTERNS
Next row (RS) K2 (4, 6) (St st edge sts), sl marker, cable over 10 sts, sl marker, k10, S2KP, k10 (now 21 sts in this section), sl marker, cable over 10 sts, sl marker, k10, S2KP, k10 (now 21 sts in this section), sl marker, cable over 10 sts, sl marker, end k2 (4, 6) (St st edge sts)—76 (80, 84) sts.
Next row P2 (4, 6) (edge sts), sl marker, cable over 10 sts, sl marker, p7, pm, work in seed st over 7 sts, pm, p7, sl marker, cable over center 10 sts, sl marker, p7, pm, work in seed st over 7 sts, pm, p7, sl marker, cable over 10 sts, sl marker, end p2 (4, 6) (edge sts). Work even until piece measures 9½"/24cm, end with a WS row.
Next (dec) row (RS) Work in pat to first 7-st St st panel, then *ssk in the first 2 sts of panel (now 6 sts rem in panel); work to 2nd St st section and rep from *, then, keeping in pat, rep from * in rem St st panels—4 sts dec. Rep dec row every 18th row 3 times

(total of 4 dec rows); at the same time, work even in pat until piece measures approx 12½ (13, 13½)"/32 (33, 34.5)cm, ending with row 4 of cable pat—60 (64, 68) sts.
Next row (RS) K2 (4, 6) (edge sts), sl marker, p2, [k2tog] 3 times, p2 (now 7 sts in this section), sl marker, work as established to center sts and sl marker, p2, [k2tog] 3 times, p2, sl marker, cont as established to last cable, and sl marker, p2, [k2tog] 3 times, p2, sl marker, end k2 (4, 6) (edge sts)—51 (55, 59) sts.
Next row P2 (4, 6) (edge sts), slip marker, work row 1 of eyelet panel over 7 sts, slip marker, work as established to center sts, slip marker, work row 1 of eyelet panel over center 7 sts, slip marker, work as established to last 9 sts, in last section, slip marker, work row 1 of eyelet panel over 7 sts, slip marker, end p2 (4, 6) (edge sts).
Cont as established until piece measures 19 (19½, 20)"/48 (49.5, 51)cm, ending with a WS row.

ARMHOLE SHAPING
Bind off 5 (6, 7) sts at beg of next RS row—46 (49, 52) sts.
Next (dec) row (RS) K1, ssk, work as set to end—45 (48, 51) sts.
Next row P2 (4, 6), work as established to last 2 (4, 6) sts, p2 (4, 6).
Rep last 2 rows 15 (17, 20) times—30 (31, 31) sts. Bind off.

RIGHT FRONT
Work as for left front, reversing all shaping and placement of dec as follows:
Dec row (RS) Work to last 2 sts of first 7-st St st panel, then *k2tog in last 2 sts of panel (now 6 sts rem in panel); work to last 2 sts of second St st section and rep from *, then, keeping in pat, rep from * in rem St st panels—4 sts dec. Beg armhole shaping one row later,

section), slip marker, cable over 10 sts, slip marker, k2 (4, 6) (edge sts)—76 (80, 84) sts.
Next row P2 (4, 6) (edge sts), slip marker, cable over 10 sts, slip marker, p7, pm, work in seed st over 7 sts, pm, p7, sl marker, cable over center 10 sts, sl marker, p7, place marker, work in seed st over 7 sts, pm, p7 sts, sl marker, cable over 10 sts, sl marker, end p2 (4, 6) (edge sts). Work even as established until sleeve measures approx 12"/30.5cm, ending with row 4 of cable pat.
Next row (RS) K2 (4, 6) (edge sts), sl marker, p2, [k2tog] 3 times, p2 (now 7 sts in this section), sl marker, work 21 sts as

established, sl marker, p2, [k2tog] 3 times, p2, sl marker, work 21 sts as established, sl marker, p2, [k2tog] 3 times, p2, sl marker, end k2 (4, 6) (edge sts)—67 (71, 75) sts.
Next row P2 (4, 6) (edge sts), sl marker, work row 1 of eyelet panel over 7 sts, sl marker, work 21 sts as established, sl marker, work row 1 of eyelet panel over center 7 sts, sl marker, work 21 sts as established, sl marker, work row 1 of eyelet panel over 7 sts, sl marker, end p2 (4, 6) (edge sts). Work even in pat until sleeve measures 17½ (18, 18½)"/44.5 (45.5, 47)cm, ending with a WS row.

and bind off last row on same row as for left front.

BACK

With larger needles, cast on 146 (152, 160) sts. Purl 1 row.

Next row (RS) K2 (5, 9) (St st edge sts), pm, work row 1 of twist cable over 10 sts, pm, [work row 1 of leaf border over 23 sts, pm] 4 times, work row 1 of twist cable over 10 sts, pm, end k2 (5, 9) (St st edge sts). Keeping in pat as established, work even until 4 reps of leaf border pattern are complete (48 rows total); end with a WS row. Piece measures approx 7½"/19cm.

CHANGE PATTERNS

Next row (RS) K2 (5, 9) (St st edge sts), sl marker, cable over 10 sts, sl marker, [k10, S2KP, k10 (now 21 sts in this section), sl marker, cable over 10 sts, sl marker] 3 times, k10, S2KP, k10 (now 21 sts in this section), sl marker, cable over 10 sts, sl marker, end k2 (5, 9) (St st edge sts)—138 (144, 152) sts.

Next row P2 (5, 9) (edge sts), sl marker, cable over 10 sts, sl marker, [p7, pm, work in seed st over 7 sts, pm, p7, sl marker, cable over center 10 sts, sl marker] 3 times, p7, pm, work in seed st over 7 sts, pm, p7, sl marker, cable over 10 sts, sl marker, end k2 (5, 9) (edge sts). Work even in pat until piece measures 9½"/24cm, ending with a WS row.

Next (dec) row (RS) Work in pat to first 7-st St st panel, *ssk in first 2 sts of panel (now 6 sts rem in panel); work to second St st section and rep from *; then, keeping in pat, rep from * in rem St st panels—8 sts dec. Rep dec row every 18th row 3 times and, at the same time, work even in pat until piece measures approx 12½ (13, 13½)"/32 (33, 34.5)cm, ending with row 4 of cable pat—106 (112, 120) sts.

Next row (RS) K2 (5, 9) (edge sts), sl marker, p2, [k2tog] 3 times, p2 (now 7 sts in this section), sl marker, [cont as established to cable sts and sl marker, p2, (k2tog) 3 times, p2, sl marker] 3 times; cont as set to last cable, and sl marker, p2, [k2tog] 3 times, p2, sl marker, end k2 (5, 9) (edge sts)—91 (97, 105) sts.

Next row (WS) P2 (5, 9) (edge sts), sl marker, work row 1 of eyelet panel over 7 sts, sl marker, [work as set to next cable st panel, sl marker, work row 1 of eyelet panel over 7 sts, sl marker] 3 times, work as set to last 9 sts, in last section, sl marker, work row 1 of eyelet panel over 7 sts, sl marker, end p2 (5, 9) (edge sts). Cont in pat, working dec in St st sections as established, until piece measures 19 (19½, 20)"/48 (49.5, 51)cm, ending with a WS row.

ARMHOLE SHAPING

Bind off 5 (6, 7) sts at beg of next 2 rows—81 (85, 91) sts.

Next (dec) row (RS) K1, ssk, work as set to last 3 sts, k2tog, k1—79 (83, 89) sts.

Next row P2, work as set to last 2 sts, p2.

Rep the last 2 rows 17 (19, 22) times—45 sts. Bind off.

FINISHING

Sew fronts and back to sleeves along raglan lines. Sew sleeve and side seams.

BUTTON BAND

On left front, with RS facing and smaller needles, pick up and knit 109 (115, 121) sts evenly along front edge. Work in garter st (k every row) for 6 rows. Bind off.

BUTTONHOLE BAND

On right front, work as for button band for 2 rows.

Next row (WS) K2, bind off 4 sts, *k12 (13, 14), bind off 4 sts; rep from * until 6 buttonholes are made, knit to end. On next row, knit, casting on 4 sts over bound-off sts. Cont as for button band.

NECK TRIM

With RS facing and smaller needles, pick up and knit 135 sts around neck opening.

Next row (WS) P2, *k1, p1; rep from * to raglan sts, p2; rep from * to last 2 sts, p2. Work 2 more rows in pat.

Next (dec) row (RS) *Work in pat to 1 st before raglan sts, k2tog, ssk; rep from *, work in pat to end—8 sts dec. Keeping raglan sts in St st, rep dec row every other row twice—111 sts. Work even until piece measures 1¼"/3cm. Bind off.

Block pieces to measurements. Weave in ends. Sew buttons opposite buttonholes.❤

9"

BACK

6 (7, 8)"

19 (19½, 20)"

30 (32, 33½)"

19 (20½, 22)"

6¼ (6½, 6½)"

7 (8)"

25 (26½, 28)"

19 (19½, 20)"

LEFT FRONT

17 (18, 18½)"

16 (17½, 18½)"

14 (15, 15¾)"

SLEEVES

17½ (18, 18½)"   6 (7, 8)"

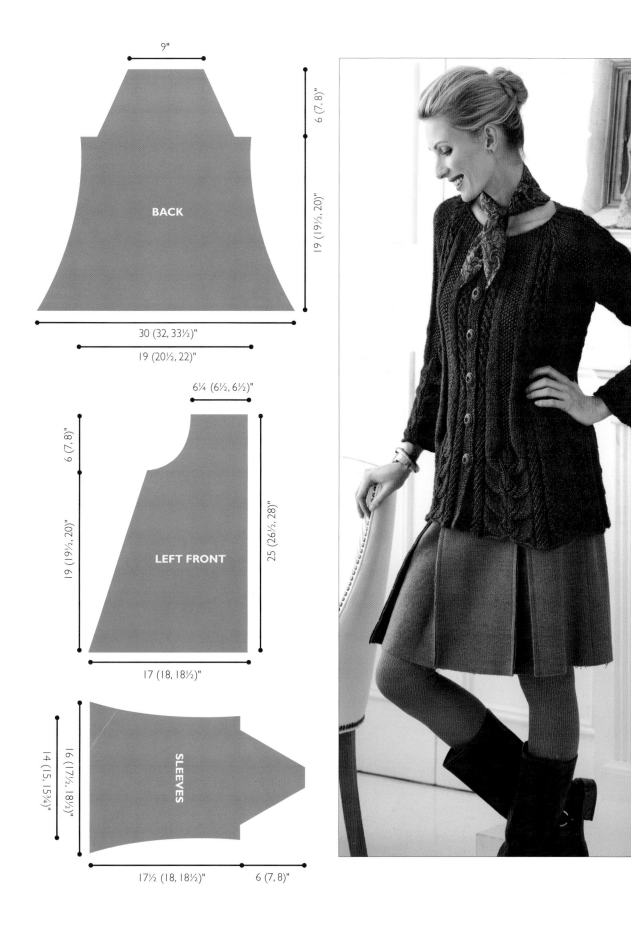

❤ TANIS GRAY

Lace infinity scarf

Wrap yourself in never-ending luxury with this luscious long cowl. Knit in lipstick red, it makes a stunning statement.

SIZE
Instructions are written for one size.

MEASUREMENTS
WIDTH Approx 8½"/21.5cm
CIRCUMFERENCE Approx 50"/127cm

MATERIALS
• 3 1¾oz/50g hanks (each approx 82yd/75m) of Be Sweet *Simply Sweet Whipped Cream* (kid mohair/wool/silk) in #803 lipstick ⑤
• Contrasting worsted weight cotton (waste yarn)
• One pair size 8 (5mm) needles *or size to obtain gauge*
• One size 10 (6mm) needle (for 3-needle bind-off)
• Size G/6 (4mm) crochet hook (for chain-st provisional cast-on)

GAUGE
18 sts to 4"/10cm and 22 rows to 5"/12.5cm over lace chart pat using size 8 (5mm) needles.
➤Take time to check gauge.

COWL
With crochet hook and waste yarn, ch 43 for chain-st provisional cast-on.
Cut yarn and draw end though lp on hook. Turn ch so bottom lps are at top and cut end is at left. With size 8 (5mm) needles, beg 2 lps from right end, then pick up and k 1 st in each of next 38 lps—38 sts.

BEG CHART PAT
Row 1 (RS) Work first 2 sts, work 11-st rep 3 times, work last 3 sts. Cont to foll chart in this way to row 10, then rep rows 1–10 twenty-one times more, or until 1yd/1m of yarn rem, end with a WS row. Leave sts on needle.

FINISHING
With RS facing, release cut end from lp of waste yarn ch. Pulling out 1 ch at a time, place 38 live sts onto size 8 (5mm) needle ready for a RS row. Join top and bottom edges using 3-needle bind-off and size 10 (6mm) needle. Block piece to measurements.❤

STITCH KEY
☐ K on RS, p on WS
⊟ P on RS, k on WS
⊠ K2tog
⊠ Ssk
Ⓞ Yarn over

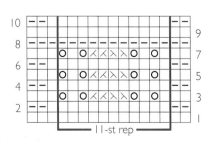

— 11-st rep —

TANIS'S STORY
Tanis was first inspired to knit at the age of eight after watching both of her grandmothers and her mother work wonders with knitting needles. A former yarn editor for *Vogue Knitting* and *Knit Simple*, Tanis now teaches knitting classes, writes knitting books, and designs for several major yarn companies. One of Tanis's grandmothers passed away due to congestive heart failure in her late 70s, and heart problems were also a significant issue for her grandfather. These close encounters with heart disease inspire Tanis to make healthy choices, such as eating five servings of fruits and veggies daily and running several times a week. She stays motivated to exercise and eat right by thinking of her newborn son and how she would like to be around to play with his children someday.

❤TANIS'S TIP
LOOK FOR WAYS TO SIMPLIFY and lighten up your favorite recipes. There are so many easy ways to create heart-healthy meals without sacrificing flavor. For example, Tanis prefers to cook with extra-virgin olive oil instead of butter. How easy is that!

 **YSOLDA TEAGUE**

Slip stitch beret

This fun and flirty beret features a simple shape that allows the subtly textured stitch pattern to shine. It's the topper to the chicest outfit.

SIZE
Instructions are written for one size.

MEASUREMENTS
CIRCUMFERENCE 20"/51cm

MATERIALS
• 1 2oz/56g ball (each approx 200yd/183m) of Lorna's Laces *Shepherd Sport* (superwash wool) in bold red (2)
• One pair size 6 (4mm) needles *or size to obtain gauge*
• Spare size 6 (4mm) needle (for 3-needle bind-off)
• Waste yarn (for provisional cast-on)

GAUGES
26 sts and 44 rows to 4"/10cm over pattern using size 6 (4mm) needles.
22 sts and 28 rows to 4"/10cm over St st using size 6 (4mm) needles.
➤Take time to check gauges.

NOTE
Beret is worked using short rows, then joined using a 3-needle bind-off.

BERET
Using provisional cast-on, cast on 51 sts.
Row 1 (RS) Knit.
Row 2 P2, *sl 2 wyib, p2; rep from * to last 13 sts, sl 2 wyib, turn.
Row 3 Sl 1 wyib, *sl 2 wyif, k2; rep from * to last 3 sts, sl 2 wyif, sl 1 wyib, turn.
Row 4 *Sl 2 wyib, p2; rep from * to last 11 sts, sl 2 wyib, turn.
Row 5 Sl 1 wyib, *sl 2 wyif, k2; rep from * to last 5 sts, sl 2 wyif, sl 1 wyib, turn.
Row 6 *Sl 2 wyib, p2; rep from * to last 9 sts, sl 2 wyib, turn.
Row 7 Sl 1 wyib, *sl 2 wyif, k2; rep from * to last 7 sts, sl 2 wyif, sl 1 wyib, turn.

Row 8 *Sl 2 wyib, p2; rep from * to last 7 sts, sl 2 wyib, turn.
Row 9 Sl 1 wyib, *sl 2 wyif, k2; rep from * to last 9 sts, sl 2 wyif, sl 1 wyib, turn.
Row 10 *Sl 2 wyib, p2; rep from * to last 5 sts, sl 2 wyib, purl to end.
Row 11 Sl 3 wyib, k1, *sl 2 wyif, k2; rep from * to last 11 sts, sl 2 wyif, sl 1 wyib, turn.
Row 12 *Sl 2 wyib, p2; rep from * to last 7 sts, sl 2 wyib, purl to end.
Row 13 Sl 3 wyib, k3, *sl 2 wyif, k2; rep from * to last 13 sts, sl 2 wyif, sl 1 wyib, turn.
Row 14 *Sl 2 wyib, p2; rep from * to last 5 sts, sl 2 wyib, purl to end.
Row 15 Sl 3 wyib, k1, *sl 2 wyif, k2; rep from * to last 15 sts, sl 2 wyif, sl 1 wyib, turn.
Row 16 *Sl 2 wyib, p2; rep from * to last 7 sts, sl 2 wyib, purl to end.
Row 17 Sl 3 wyib, k3, *sl 2 wyif, k2; rep from * to last 17 sts, sl 2 wyif, sl 1 wyib, turn.
Row 18 *Sl 2 wyib, p2; rep from * to last 5 sts, sl 2 wyib, purl to end.
Row 19 Sl 3 wyib, k1, *sl 2 wyif, k2; rep from * to last 19 sts, sl 2 wyif, turn.
Row 20 Sl 1 wyif, *sl 2 wyib, p2; rep from * to last 5 sts, sl 2 wyib, purl to end.
Row 21 Sl 3 wyib, k3, *sl 2 wyif, k2; rep from * to last 17 sts, sl 2 wyif, turn.
Row 22 Sl 1 wyif, *sl 2 wyib, p2; rep from * to last 7 sts, sl 2 wyib, purl to end.

YSOLDA'S STORY
Growing up in Scotland, home to one of the highest rates of heart disease in Europe, Ysolda saw firsthand the toll of a culture of heavy drinking, smoking, and fried foods—all major contributors to heart disease. Several members of Ysolda's own family have undergone bypass surgery, and she hopes that *Knit Red* will help dispel the stereotype that heart disease affects only older men who drink and smoke excessively. As an independent designer and enthusiastic globetrotter, Ysolda spends a lot of time on the road and finds it a challenge to maintain a healthy lifestyle. She tries to eat as many veggies as she can, avoids processed foods, and never says no to a home-cooked meal. Ysolda loves to indulge in a swim anytime she stays at a hotel with a pool. At home in her hilly city, Ysolda enjoys running errands on foot. Since she works mostly from home, she finds that taking a quick trip to the market is a great way to get out of the house and into the open air.

Row 23 Sl 3 wyib, k1, *sl 2 wyif, k2; rep from * to last 15 sts, sl 2 wyif, turn.

Row 24 Sl 1 wyif, *sl 2 wyib, p2; rep from * to last 5 sts, sl 2 wyib, purl to end.

Row 25 Sl 3 wyib, k3, *sl 2 wyif, k2; rep from * to last 13 sts, sl 2 wyif, turn.

Row 26 Sl 1 wyif, *sl 2 wyib, p2; rep from * to last 7 sts, sl 2 wyib, purl to end.

Row 27 Sl 3 wyib, k1, *sl 2 wyif, k2; rep from * to last 11 sts, sl 2 wyif, turn.

Row 28 Sl 1 wyif, *sl 2 wyib, p2; rep from * to last 5 sts, sl 2 wyib, purl to end.

Row 29 Sl 3 wyib, k3, *sl 2 wyif, k2; rep from * to last 9 sts, sl 2 wyif, turn.

Row 30 Sl 1 wyif, *sl 2 wyib, p2; rep from * to last 7 sts, sl 2 wyib, sl 1 wyif, turn.

Row 31 *Sl 2 wyif, k2; rep from * to last 7 sts, sl 2 wyif, turn.

Row 32 Sl 1 wyif, *sl 2 wyib, p2; rep from * to last 9 sts, sl 2 wyib, sl 1 wyif, turn.

Row 33 *Sl 2 wyif, k2; rep from * to last 5 sts, sl 2 wyif, turn.

Row 34 Sl 1 wyif, *sl 2 wyib, p2; rep from * to last 11 sts, sl 2 wyib, sl 1 wyif, turn.

Row 35 *Sl 2 wyif, k2; rep from * to last 3 sts, sl 2 wyif, turn.

Row 36 Sl 1 wyif, *sl 2 wyib, p2; rep from * to last 13 sts, sl 2 wyib, sl 1 wyif, turn.

Row 37 *Sl 2 wyif, k2; rep from * to last 5 sts, sl 2 wyif, k to end.

Rep rows 2–37 eight times more.

FINISHING

Undo provisional cast-on and place sts on spare needle.
With RS tog, join using 3-needle bind-off.
Use tail to pull center sts tight.
Weave in ends. Block to shape using a dinner plate or circle of cardboard. ❤

❤ YSOLDA'S TIP

IF YOU LOVE TO BAKE, as Ysolda does, try using unrefined sugars and whole-wheat flour to keep those cakes and cookies as healthy as they can be. A sweet treat doesn't have to sabotage your healthy diet!

DEBORAH NORVILLE

Cabled knee-highs

Deborah and the Premier Yarns Design Team created these bright and cozy socks. Knit in soft acrylic, they make an easy-care gift for everyone on your list.

SIZE
Instructions are written for size Medium.

MEASUREMENTS
CALF CIRCUMFERENCE
11"/28cm (slightly stretched)
FOOT CIRCUMFERENCE
7½"/19cm
LENGTH (CUFF TO HEEL)
15½"/39.5cm
LENGTH (HEEL TO TOE)
9"/23cm

MATERIALS
• 2 4oz/113g balls (each approx 203yd/186m) of Deborah Norville Collection Everyday Soft Worsted Solids (acrylic) in #ED100-07 really red (4)
• One set (4) size 5 (3.75mm) double-pointed needles (dpns) *or size to obtain gauge*
• Cable needle (cn)
• Stitch marker

GAUGE
22 sts and 26 rnds to 4"/10cm over cable pat st using size 5 (3.75mm) dpns.
➤ Take time to check gauge.

STITCH GLOSSARY
6-st RC Sl 3 sts to cn and hold to back, k3, k3 from cn.
6-st LC Sl 3 sts to cn and hold to front, k3, k3 from cn.

CABLE AND RIB PATTERN
Rnd 1 Needle 1: K1, p2, k2, p2, 6-st RC, p2, k1; Needle 2: K1, p2, 6-st LC, p2, 6-st RC, p2, k1; Needle 3: K1, p2, 6-st LC, p2, k2, p2, k1.
Rnds 2–6 Needle 1: K1, p2, k2, p2, k6, p2, k1; Needle 2: K1, p2, k6, p2, k6, p2, k1; Needle 3: K1, p2, k6, p2, k2, p2, k1.
Rep rnds 1–6 for cable and rib pat.

DEBORAH'S STORY
You may know Deborah as the longtime anchor of the television news show *Inside Edition,* but she also happens to be an avid knitter and designer and has her own line of yarns. For Deborah, knitting is an essential part of her life and her health. Not only is it fun and relaxing, but she cites Harvard Medical School studies that show that the repetitive motion of knitting actually helps lower stress and reduce blood pressure! Deborah grew up in the South, where fried foods were a large part of the local cuisine and culture, and heart disease runs in her family. After losing her grandfather to an aneurysm when he was 68 and watching her father struggle with an array of heart disease–related issues, including heart blockages, a quintuple bypass surgery, and high cholesterol, Deborah has made it her goal to live as heart-healthy a lifestyle as possible. She likes to cook with fresh vegetables, limits the amount of red meat she and her family consume, and staves off the munchies in between meals with a handful of protein-rich almonds.

The cable and rib pattern follows the curves of the calf, creating an eye-catching design detail.

SOCK

CUFF

Cast on 52 sts.
Divide sts as foll: 16 sts on Needle 1; 20 sts on Needle 2; 16 sts on Needle 3.
(Needles 1 and 3 hold the heel sts and Needle 2 holds the instep sts.) Join, taking care not to twist sts on needles, pm for beg of rnds. Cont in k2, p2 rib as foll:
Rnd 1 K1, *p2, k2; rep from * around, end p2, k1.
Rep rnd 1 until piece measures 1"/2.5cm from beg.

LEG

Cont in cable and rib pat and work even for 4 rnds.

CALF SHAPING

Working new sts in k2, p2 rib, inc 1 st at beg and end of next rnd, then every other rnd 5 times more—64 sts. Work even in pat as established until piece measures approx 5¾"/14.5cm from beg. Dec 1 st at beg and end of next rnd, then every other rnd 9 times more—44 sts. Work even in pat as established until piece measures approx 13"/33cm from beg.
Next (dec) rnd Work around, dec 4 sts evenly spaced across Needles 1 and 3—40 sts; 10 sts each on Needles 1 and 3 (heel), and 20 sts on Needle 2 (instep).

BEG HEEL FLAP

Note Heel flap is worked back and forth on one needle over 20 sts; rem 20 sts on Needle 2 are on hold.
Row 1 (RS) *Sl 1 purlwise, k1; rep from * to end.
Row 2 Sl 1, purl to end.
Rep rows 1 and 2 seven times more, then row 1 once.

TURN HEEL

Row 1 (WS) Sl 1, p11, p2tog, p1; turn.
Row 2 (RS) Sl 1, k5, k2tog, k1; turn.
Row 3 Sl 1, p6, p2tog, p1; turn.
Row 4 Sl 1, k7, k2tog, k1; turn.
Cont in this manner, working 1 more st before dec every row until all sts are worked—12 heel sts. Cut yarn.

GUSSET

Next rnd With RS facing and Needle 1, pick up and k 8 sts along side edge of heel flap; work in cable and rib pat across 20 instep sts on Needle 2, then with new Needle 3, pick up and k 8 sts along opposite side edge of heel flap, then k6 heel sts—48 sts. Join and pm for beg of rnds (center back of heel).
Dec rnd Needle 1: Knit to last 3 sts, k2tog, k1; Needle 2: Work in cable and rib pat; Needle 3: K1, ssk, knit to end—46 sts.
Next rnd Work even in pat. Rep last 2 rnds 3 times more—40 sts.

FOOT

Work even in pats as established (St st on Needles 1 and 3 and cable and rib pat on Needle 2) until foot measures approx 2"/5cm less than desired length from heel to toe. (Try on sock to ensure the correct length.)

TOE

Dec rnd Needle 1: Knit to last 3 sts, k2tog, k1; Needle 2: K1, ssk, knit to last 3 sts, k2tog, k1; Needle 3: K1, ssk, knit to end—36 sts.
Next rnd Knit. Rep last 2 rnds 5 times more—16 sts. Cut yarn. Graft toe sts using Kitchener st. ♥

Red roses shrug

Feel the power of flowers in this gorgeous chenille shrug embellished with sumptuous roses. It's constructed as a simple rectangle that is seamed to create sleeves.

▰▰▰▱

SIZES
Instructions are written for size X-Small/Small. Changes for Medium/Large, 1X/2X are in parentheses. (Shown in size X-Small/Small.)

MEASUREMENTS
ACROSS BACK
20 (24, 28)"/51 (61, 71)cm
UPPER ARM
13 (15, 17)"/33 (38, 43)cm

MATERIALS
• 11 (14, 16) 1¾oz/50g balls (each approx 61yd/56m) of Muench Yarns *Touch Me* (rayon microfiber/wool) in #3600 ④
• One pair each size 8 (5mm) needles *or size to obtain gauge*
• Size 7 (4.5mm) crochet hook
• 1½yd/1.5m of ⅜"/10mm wide matching grosgrain ribbon
• Matching sewing thread
• Sewing needle

GAUGE
19 sts to 5"/12.5cm and 22 rows to 4"/10cm over St st using size 8 (5mm) needles.
➤ Take time to check gauge.

NOTE
Shrug is made in one piece from right sleeve edge to left sleeve edge.

STITCH GLOSSARY
kf&b Inc 1 by knitting into the front and back of the next st.

STOCKINETTE STITCH
Row 1 (RS) Knit.
Row 2 Purl.
Rep rows 1 and 2 for St st.

REVERSE STOCKINETTE STITCH
Row 1 (RS) Purl.
Row 2 Knit.
Rep rows 1 and 2 for reverse St st.

SHRUG
Beg at right sleeve edge, cast on 98 (114, 130) sts.

RUFFLE AND EYELETS
Row 1 (RS) Knit.
Row 2 Purl.
Row 3 Knit.
Row (dec) 4 (WS) P1, *p2tog; rep from *, end p1—50 (58, 66) sts.
Row 5 Knit.
Row 6 Purl.
Row 7 Knit.
Row (eyelets) 8 (WS) *P1, yo, p2tog; rep from *, end p 2 (1, 0).

▲ Arrange the roses as in the photos or in your own configuration.

Cont right sleeve, back and beg left sleeve as foll: work in St st for 26 (28, 30) rows, [work in reverse St st for 26 (28, 30) rows, work in St st for 26 (28, 30) rows] 5 times, end with a WS row.

EYELETS AND RUFFLE
Row (eyelets) 1 (RS) *K1, yo, k2tog; rep from *, end k 2 (1, 0).
Row 2 Purl.
Row 3 Knit.
Row 4 Purl.
Row (inc) 5 (RS) K1, *kf&b; rep from *, end k1—98 (114, 130) sts.
Row 6 Purl.
Row 7 Knit.
Row 8 Purl. Bind off knitwise (left sleeve edge).

SMALL ROSES
[MAKE 3 (5, 5)]
Cast on 10 sts.
Row 1 (RS) Knit.
Row 2 and all WS rows Purl.
Row 3 *Kf&b; rep from * to end—20 sts.
Row 5 Rep row 3—40 sts. Bind off purlwise.

MEDIUM ROSES
[MAKE 9 (11, 11)]
Cast on 10 sts.
Row 1 (RS) Knit.
Row 2 and all WS rows Purl.
Row 3 *Kf&b; rep from * to end—20 sts.
Row 5 Rep row 3—40 sts.
Row 7 Rep row 3—80 sts.
Row 8 Purl. Bind off knitwise.

LARGE ROSES
[MAKE 3 (3, 5)]
Cast on 15 sts.
Row 1 (RS) Knit.
Row 2 and all WS rows Purl.
Row 3 *Kf&b; rep from * to end—30 sts.
Row 5 Rep row 3—60 sts.
Row 7 Rep row 3—120 sts.
Row 8 Purl. Bind off knitwise.

FINISHING
Sew a 19"/23cm sleeve seam each side.

EDGING
With RS facing and crochet hook, join yarn with a sl st in top of right sleeve seam.
Rnd 1 (RS) Ch 1, making sure that work lies flat, sc evenly around entire edge, join rnd with a sl st in first sc. Fasten off.

ROSES
To make each rose, roll first 1"/2.5cm of sts to form center, then secure on cast-on edge using sewing needle and thread. Cont to spiral length around center, securing along cast-on edge as you go. Referring to photo, arrange and pin roses as shown or as desired. Sew in place using sewing needle and thread. Cut ribbon in half. Beg and ending at sleeve seam, weave ribbon through eyelets. Tie in a bow, then trim ends at an angle to desired length. ❤

→ = Direction of work

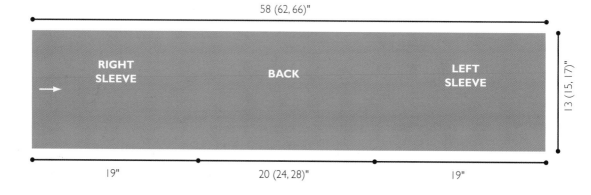

58 (62, 66)"

RIGHT SLEEVE   BACK   LEFT SLEEVE

13 (15, 17)"

19"   20 (24, 28)"   19"

♥ **DANIELA JOHANNSENOVA**

Graphic tunic

Unusual construction, an asymmetrical design, and luxe yarns add up to one show-stopping creation. The easy fit makes it flattering for all figures.

◼◼◼▭

SIZES
Instructions are written for size Small. Changes for Medium and Large are in parentheses. (Shown in size Small.)

MEASUREMENTS
BUST 36 (40, 44)"/91.5 (101.5, 111.5)cm
LENGTH 26½ (27½, 28½)"/67 (70, 72.5)cm
UPPER ARM 12 (14, 16)"/30.5 (35.5, 40.5)cm

MATERIALS
• 1 (2, 2) 2¾ oz/80g balls (each approx 400yd/366m) of Artyarns *Rhapsody Light* (silk/kid mohair) in dark red (A) ◼
• 1 (1, 2) 2¾ oz/80g balls (each approx 400yd/366m) of Artyarns *Rhapsody Light* (silk/kid mohair) in each of medium dark red (B), medium red (C), pale red (D)
• 2 1¾oz/50g balls (each approx 114yd/104m) of Artyarns *Beaded Mohair and Sequins* (silk with glass beads and sequins/kid mohair) in #300 red w/ gold (E) ◼
• Size 4 (3.5mm) circular needles, 29"/75cm and 16"/40cm long, *or size to obtain gauge*

• One set (5) size 4 (3.5mm) double-pointed needles (dpns)
• Size 6 (4mm) circular needle, 29"/75cm long
• Size 9 (5.5mm) circular needle 29"/75cm long
• Stitch markers
• Stitch holders or waste yarn

GAUGE
22 sts and 28 rows to 4"/10cm over St st with A and size 4 (3.5mm) needles.
➤ Take time to check gauge.

TUNIC
BLOCK 1
With longer size 4 (3.5mm) circular needle and A, cast on 110 (120, 132) sts. Pm after 55 (60, 66) sts (mark side edge of tunic). Work in St st for 1½"/4cm, end with a WS row.
Next (inc) row K1, M1, knit to last st, M1, k1—2 sts inc. Cont in St st, rep inc row every 6th row 11 times, then every 10th row twice—138 (148, 160) sts. Work even until piece measures 19"/48cm. K 4 rows. Bind off.

BLOCK 2
With longer size 4 (3.5mm) circular needle and D, cast on 70 (82, 94) sts.
Work as for block 1, pm after 35 (41, 47) sts (mark side edge of tunic)—98 (110, 122) sts.

VERTICAL BEADED STRIPE 1 (MAKE 2)
Note Stripe is worked vertically between the side edges of blocks 1 and 2, joining as work progresses.
With size 9 (5.5mm) needle and E, cast on 10 sts.
Row 1 (WS) Place edge st of last row of block 2 on left needle, k2tog (st from block 2 and first st of stripe), [k1, p1] 4 times, sl 1, place edge st of last row of block 1 on left needle, psso—10 sts.
Row 2 Sl 1, [p1, k1] 4 times, sl 1.
Rep rows 1 and 2 to top of blocks, changing to size 6 (4mm) needle approx one-third of the way up the blocks, then to longer size 4 (3.5mm) circular needle for the final one-third. Place sts on holder. Rep for back. Leave sts on needle.

HORIZONTAL BEADED STRIPE
Rnd 1 With RS facing and longer size 4 (3.5mm) circular needle, cont with E, pick up and knit 69 (81, 93) sts across cast-on edge of block 2, work [k1, p1] 5 times across top of next beaded stripe, pick up and knit 109 (119, 131) sts across cast-on edge of block 1—198 (220, 244) sts. Join, pm for beg of rnd.

Rnd 2 [P1, k1] 5 times, p1, [k2tog, p1, k1, p1] 13 (15, 17) times, [k1, p1] 7 (8, 10) times, [k2tog, p1, k1, p1] 21 (23, 25) times, k1, p1, k1—164 (182, 202) sts.

Rnd 3 *K1, p1; rep from * around.

Rnd 4 *P1, k1; rep from * around. Rep last 2 rnds 5 times, then work rnd 3 once more.

VETICAL BEADED STRIPE 2

Next row (RS) Place all sts except the 10 vertical stripe sts on front on holders. Working on 10 stripe sts only, cont in seed st as established for 12 (14, 16)"/ 30.5 (35.5, 40.5)cm, slipping the first st of each row. Place sts on holder and cut yarn, leaving long tail for sewing.

Sew to top of horizontal stripe on the back.

SLEEVE 1

Note Change to shorter needles, then dpns, as needed.

With size 4 (3.5mm) needle and B, pick up and knit 64 (76, 88) sts along the edge of vertical stripe 2, above block 2.

Row 1 (WS) Sl 1, purl to last st, p2tog (last st and first st from horizontal stripe on holder), turn.

Row 2 Sl 1, knit to last st, sl 1, k1 from horizontal stripe on holder, psso, turn.

Rows 3 and 4 Rep rows 1 and 2.

Row 5 Sl 1, purl to last st, p3tog (last st and next 2 sts from horizontal stripe on holder), turn.

Row 6 Sl 1, knit to the last st, sl 1, k2tog from horizontal stripe on holder, psso, turn.

Rep rows 1–6 until all sts from horizontal stripe are used. Join, pm to mark beg of rnd.

Work even in St st for 4"/10cm.

Next (dec) rnd K1, ssk, knit to last 3 sts, k2tog, k1—2 sts dec. Rep dec rnd every 5th rnd 5

times, then every 4th rnd 8 times—36 (48, 60) sts. Work even until piece measures 14½ (15, 15½)"/37 (38, 39.5)cm from join. Join a strand of E.

Next rnd Knit.

Next rnd Purl. Bind off knitwise.

SLEEVE 2

BACK HALF

With size 4 (3.5mm) needles and C, pick up and knit 32 (38, 44) sts on back half of vertical stripe 2, above block 1.

Row 1 (WS) Sl 1, purl to last st, p2tog (last st and first st from horizontal stripe on holder), turn.

Row 2 Sl 1, knit to end.

Rep rows 1 and 2 a total of 28 (33, 38) times.

FRONT HALF

With size 4 (3.5mm) needles and C, pick up and knit 32 (38, 44) sts on front half of vertical stripe 2, above block 1.

Row 1 (WS) Sl 1, purl to end, turn.

Row 2 Sl 1, knit to last st, sl 1, k1 from horizontal stripe on holder, psso, turn.

Rep rows 1 and 2 a total of 28 (33, 38) times. Cont working across all sts (both halves) as follows:

Next row Sl 1, purl to last st of back half, p2tog (last st and first st from horizontal stripe on holder), turn.

Next row Sl 1, knit to last st, ssk (last st and first st from horizontal stripe on holder), turn.

Rep last 2 rows until all sts from horizontal stripe are used.

Join and finish as for sleeve 1.

FINISHING

Block pieces to measurements. Weave in ends. Sew edge of neckline slightly narrower if desired. ❤

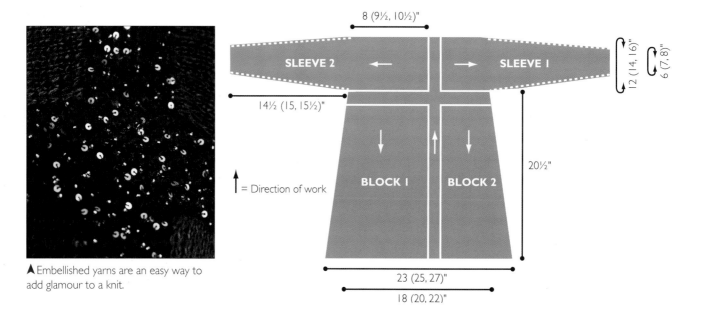

▲ Embellished yarns are an easy way to add glamour to a knit.

8 (9½, 10½)"

SLEEVE 2 ← → SLEEVE 1

12 (14, 16)"

6 (7, 8)"

14½ (15, 15½)"

↑ = Direction of work

BLOCK 1   BLOCK 2

20½"

23 (25, 27)"

18 (20, 22)"

Multipattern mittens

These densely textured handwarmers are a festival of stitches, including cables, bobbles, a slip-stitch palm, and a chevron-stitch cuff. Originally designed for *Vogue Knitting*, they have been reinvented in Flood's newest yarn, *Loft*.

■—■■■

SIZE
Instructions are written for size Medium.

MEASUREMENTS
HAND CIRCUMFERENCE
7½"/19cm
LENGTH OF CUFF
3"/7.5cm

MATERIALS
• 1 1¾oz/50g hank (each approx 275yd/252m) of Brooklyn Tweed *Loft* (American wool) in #05 long johns ❶
• One set (5) size 3 (3.25mm) double-pointed needles (dpns) *or size to obtain gauge*
• Cable needle (cn)
• Stitch markers

GAUGE
32 sts and 40 rnds to 4"/10cm over St st using size 3 (3.25mm) dpns.
➤ Take time to check gauge.

NOTE
To work in the rnd, always read charts from right to left.

STITCH GLOSSARY
2-st RPC Sl 1 to cn, hold to *back*, k1 tbl, p1 from cn.
2-st LPC Sl 1 to cn, hold to *front*, p1, k1 tbl from cn.
4-st RC Sl 2 to cn, hold to *back*, k2, k2 from cn.
4-st LC Sl 2 to cn, hold to *front*, k2, k2 from cn.
4-st RPC Sl 2 to cn, hold to *back*, k2, p2 from cn.
4-st LPC Sl 2 to cn, hold to *front*, p2, k2 from cn.
5-st LPC Sl 2 to cn, hold to *front*, k2, p1, then k2 from cn.
Make bobble (MB) [K1, p1, k1, p1, k1] in same st—5 sts; then pass the 4th, 3rd, 2nd, and first sts, one at a time, over the last st made.

LEFT MITTEN
CUFF
With dpns, cast on 54 sts and divide sts over 4 needles. Join, taking care not to twist sts on needles, pm for beg of rnds.

BEG CHART 1
Rnd 1 Work 6-st rep of chart 9 times. Cont to work chart in this manner through rnd 37.
Next rnd Knit.
Next (inc) rnd Sl 1 wyib, p3, sl 1 wyib, [M1, k4] 7 times, M1, k1, sl 1 wyib, p3, sl 1 wyib, [M1, k3] 4 times, M1, k2, sl 1 wyib, M1—68 sts.

BEG CHART 2
Beg and end as indicated for left mitten, work rnds 1–26 of chart 2.

Rnd 27 Work to last 12 sts, place these 12 sts on scrap yarn for thumb, cast on 10 sts—66 sts. Join and cont to work through rnd 81—40 sts.

SADDLE CLOSING
Divide sts over needles as foll: first 5 sts on first needle (saddle), next 15 sts on 2nd needle (backside), next 5 sts on scrap yarn (saddle), last 15 sts on 3rd needle (palmside). Work back and forth over the 5 sts of saddle, using a 4th needle as foll:
Row 1 (RS) Sl first st, p3, ssk last st tog with next st on 2nd needle; turn.
Row 2 Sl first st, p3, purl tog last st with next st on 3rd needle; turn. Rep these 2 rows, dec 1 st from either front or back of mitten at end of each row until all sts on needles 2 and 3 have been used—10 sts. Place sts on scrap yarn onto dpn and bind off saddles using 3-needle bind-off.

THUMB
Beg at outer edge of palm, pick up and k 12 sts along 10 cast-on sts as foll: k into front and back of first st to pick up 2 sts, pick up 1 in each of next 8 sts, k into front and back of last st to pick up 2 sts, pm for beg of rnd, sl 12 sts from scrap yarn to 2 more dpns, divide for 8 sts on each dpn. Join to work in rnds.

JARED'S STORY
Brooklyn Tweed blogger and designer Jared Flood recently launched his own line of gorgeous American-made yarns. An entrepreneur and creator of striking knitwear, he is also one active, health-conscious guy. About two years ago, Jared changed his dietary habits significantly and tells us it was one of the best choices he ever made. By preparing about 90 percent of his meals from scratch, Jared not only knows exactly what his daily meals contain, but also hones his culinary skills. He likes to cook with extra-virgin olive oil and peanut oil instead of butter, eats as much fish as he can, and whips up fresh fruit smoothies almost every day. Of course exercise is just as important as diet, and Jared makes an effort to go for a run three to four times a week.

♥ JARED'S TIP
CHALLENGE YOURSELF to try one new recipe each week. Cooking, like knitting, is a tactile art and can be just as addictive. Buy a cookbook of heart-healthy recipes, peruse the Internet, or ask your mom for one of her famous recipes. In this age of information, there is an endless supply of cooking inspiration!

CHART 2

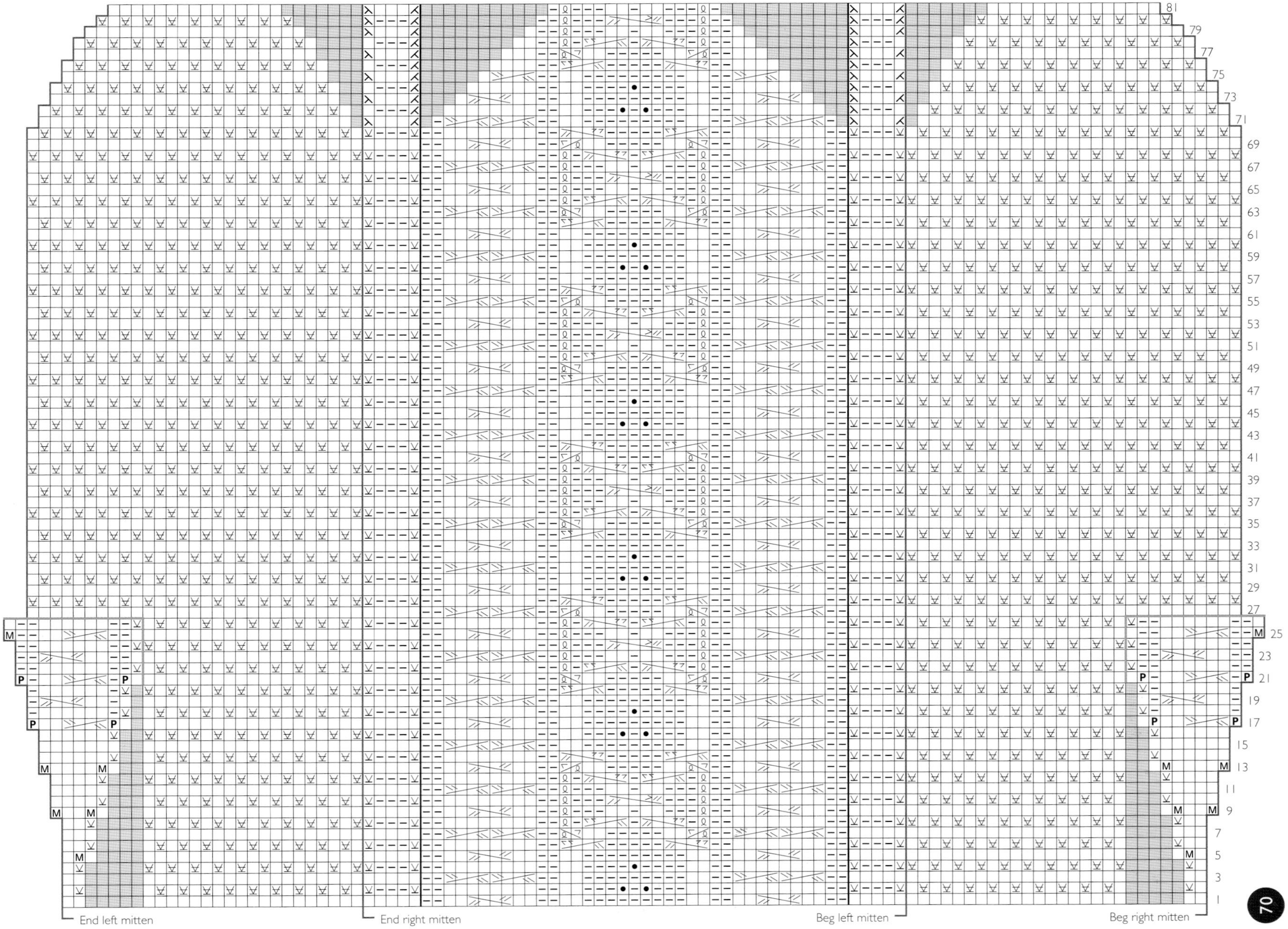

End left mitten

End right mitten

Beg left mitten

Beg right mitten

1 3 5 7 9 11 13 15 17 19 21 23 25 27 29 31 33 35 37 39 41 43 45 47 49 51 53 55 57 59 61 63 65 67 69 71 73 75 77 79 81

M P P M M M P P M K K M M K M P P M

CHART I

6 sts

CHART 3

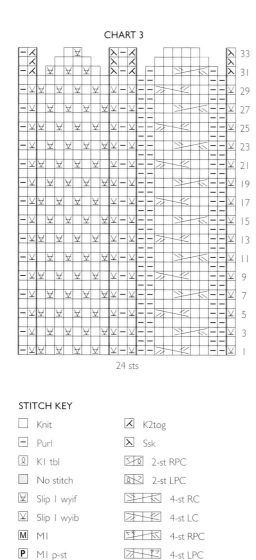

24 sts

STITCH KEY

☐	Knit	⊠	K2tog
⊟	Purl	⊠	Ssk
⍉	K1 tbl		2-st RPC
▦	No stitch		2-st LPC
⍦	Slip 1 wyif		4-st RC
⍀	Slip 1 wyib		4-st LC
M	M1		4-st RPC
P	M1 p-st		4-st LPC
•	Make bobble		5-st LPC

BEG CHART 3
Work rnds 1–33 of chart—12 sts.
Next (dec) rnd [K2tog] 6 times—6 sts. Cut yarn, leaving a 6"/15cm tail. Thread tail into tapestry needle, then thread through rem sts. Pull tog tightly and secure end.

RIGHT MITTEN
CUFF
Work as for left mitten through rnd 37.
Next rnd Knit.
Next (inc) rnd M1, sl 1 wyib, k1,

[M1, k3] 4 times, M1, k1, sl 1 wyib, p3, sl 1 wyib, [M1, k4] 7 times, M1, k1, sl 1 wyib, p3, sl 1 wyib—68 sts.

BEG CHART 2
Beg and end as indicated for right mitten, work rnds 1–26 of chart 2.
Rnd 27 Sl first 12 sts to scrap yarn, cast on 10 sts, work to end—66 sts. Work through rnd 81—40 sts.

SADDLE CLOSING
Divide sts over needles as foll:

first 15 sts on first needle (palmside), next 5 sts on 2nd needle (saddle), next 15 sts on 3rd needle (backside), last 5 sts on scrap yarn (saddle).
Join yarn to work back and forth over the 5 sts of saddle, using a 4th needle as foll:
Row 1 (RS) Sl first st, p3, ssk last st tog with next st on 3rd needle; turn.
Row 2 Sl first st, p3, purl tog last st with next st on first needle; turn. Rep these 2 rows, dec 1 st from either front or back of mitten at end of each row until

all sts on needles 2 and 3 have been used—10 sts. Place sts on scrap yarn onto dpn and bind off saddles using 3-needle bind-off.

THUMB
Beg at center of palm, and pick up 12 sts in same manner as left thumb, pm for beg of rnd, sl 12 sts from scrap yarn to 2 more dpns, divide for 8 sts on each dpn. Join to work in rnds. Work foll chart 3 and complete as for left thumb.♥

♥ **KRISTEN ASHBAUGH-HELMREICH**

Greenmarket tote

This sturdy cotton tote is as stylish as it is practical. Stash it in your purse or your car so you always have it handy.

▬ ▬ ▬ ▬

MEASUREMENTS
Approx 15½"/39.5cm wide × 18"/45.5cm high (excluding handles)

MATERIALS
• 3 3½oz/100g hanks (each approx 140yd/128m) of Plymouth *Fantasy Naturale* (mercerized cotton) in #3611 red (**4**)
• Contrasting worsted weight cotton (waste yarn)
• Sizes 8 and 9 (5 and 5.5mm) circular needles, 24"/60cm long *or size to obtain gauge*
• One set (4) size 8 (5mm) double-pointed needles (dpns)
• Size G/6 (4mm) crochet hook (for chain-st provisional cast-on)
• Stitch markers

GAUGE
12 sts and 20 rnds to 4"/10cm over heart lace pat st using larger circular needle.
➤ Take time to check gauge.

STITCH GLOSSARY
SK3P Slip 1, knit 3 together, pass slip stitch over the knit 3 together—3 stitches have been decreased.
kf&b Inc 1 by knitting into the front and back of the next st.

TOTE
BOTTOM
With crochet hook and waste yarn, ch 13 for chain-st provisional cast-on. Cut yarn and draw end though lp on hook. Turn ch so bottom lps are at top and cut end is at left. With dpns, beg 2 lps from right end, then, leaving a long tail for sewing, pick up and k 1 st in each of next 8 lps—8 sts. Divide sts over 3 needles. Join, taking care not to twist sts on needles, pm for beg of rnds. Cont in garter st (knit one rnd, purl one rnd) as foll:
Rnd (inc) 1 [K1, kf&b] 4 times—12 sts. Divide sts over 3 needles.
Rnd 2 and all even rnds Purl.
Rnd (inc) 3 [K1, kf&b] 6 times—18 sts. **Rnd (inc) 5** [K2, kf&b] 6 times—24 sts. **Rnd (inc) 7** [K3, kf&b] 6 times—30 sts. **Rnd (inc) 9** [K4, kf&b] 6 times—36 sts. **Rnd (inc) 11** [K5, kf&b] 6 times—42 sts. **Rnd (inc) 13** [K6, kf&b] 6 times—48 sts. **Rnd (inc) 15** [K7, kf&b] 6 times—54 sts. **Rnd (inc) 17** [K8, kf&b] 6 times—60 sts. **Rnd (inc) 19** [K9, kf&b] 6 times—66 sts. **Rnd (inc) 21** [K10, kf&b] 6 times—72 sts. **Rnd (inc) 23** [K11, kf&b] 6 times—78 sts. **Rnd (inc) 25** [K12, kf&b] 6 times—84 sts. Change to smaller circular needle. **Rnd (inc) 27** [K13, kf&b] 6 times—90 sts. **Rnd (inc) 29** [K14, kf&b] 6 times—96 sts.

SIDES
Next 3 rnds Work in garter st. Change to larger circular needle. Cont in heart lace pat st as foll:
Rnd 1 *Yo, k2tog, k3, yo, k1, yo, k3, SKP, yo, k1; rep from * around.

Rnd 2 and all even rnds Knit.
Rnd 3 *K1, yo, k4tog, yo, k3, yo, SK3P, yo, k2; rep from * around.
Rnd 5 *K1, k2tog, yo, k5, yo, SKP, k2; rep from * around. **Rnd 7** *K2tog, yo, k7, yo, SKP, k1; rep from * around; drop rnd marker, sl first st on LH needle to RH needle, pm for new beg of rnd.
Rnd 9 *Yo, k9, yo, SK2P; rep from * around. **Rnd 10** Knit. Rep rnds 1–10 four times more, then rnds 1–4 once.

TOP BORDER AND HANDLES
Change to smaller circular needle. Cont in garter st as foll:
Rnds 1 and 3 Purl. **Rnds 2 and 4** Knit. **Rnd (dec) 5** *P14, p2tog; rep from * around—90 sts. **Rnds 6 and 8** Knit. **Rnds 7 and 9** Purl
Rnd (handle openings) 10 K15, bind off next 15 sts, knit until there are 30 sts on RH needle, bind off next 15 sts, k15.
Rnd (handles) 11 P15, cast on 30 sts, p30, cast on 30 sts, p15—120 sts. **Rnds 12, 14, 16, 18 and 20** Knit. **Rnds 13, 15, 17, 19 and 21** Purl. Bind off all sts knitwise.

FINISHING
Thread beg tail at bottom of bag into yarn needle. With RS facing, release cut end from lp of waste yarn ch. Pulling out 1 ch at a time, place 8 live sts onto yarn needle. Pull tog tightly to close opening, then secure end. ♥

KRISTEN'S STORY
Kristen is an up-and-coming designer with a talent for combining function with style in all of her designs. With a family history of heart disease and low blood pressure, and a propensity for high cholesterol, Kristen keeps her health at the top of her priority list. Kristen's father has suffered from the effects of heart disease for many years and has undergone both quadruple bypass surgery and a valve replacement. Kristen enjoys spending time outdoors. The owner of a high-energy terrier mix, she takes at least one half-hour walk daily, which helps keep both of them fit and happy. Diet is just as important for Kristen. She and her husband tend to eat mostly home-cooked vegetarian meals, so that when they do eat out occasionally, they can treat themselves to a nice steak or enjoy a slice of bacon.

♥ **KRISTEN'S TIP**
MAKE FRUITS AND VEGETABLES AN INTEGRAL PART OF YOUR DIET.
Kristen likes to start her morning off with both by enjoying a scrumptious smoothie made with fresh fruit and leafy greens, blended with low-fat yogurt.

One-shoulder tunic

This striking tunic is knit in two pieces from side to side, starting with the sleeve. The mesh stitch pattern gives it a light feel.

SIZES
Instructions are written for size Small. Changes for Medium and Large are in parentheses. (Shown in size Small.)

MEASUREMENTS
BUST 34 (38, 42)"/86.5 (96.5, 106.5)cm
LENGTH 27¾ (28½, 29)"/ 70.5 (72.5, 73.5)cm

MATERIALS
• 3 (4, 4) 3½ oz/100g balls (each approx 218yd/200m) of Cornelia Hamilton *Heaven's Hand Wool Classic* (wool) in #11655 crimson (4)
• One pair size 10½ (6.5mm) needles *or size to obtain gauge.*

GAUGE
11 sts to 4"/10cm over openwork pattern using size 10½ (6.5mm) needles.
➤ Take time to check gauge.

OPENWORK PATTERN
Row 1 *Yo, sl 1 purlwise, k1, psso; rep from * across.
Rep row 1 for openwork pat.

NOTES
1) Yarnover at beg of each row is worked by placing the yarn over the right-hand needle before working the first st of the row.
2) Piece is worked from side to side. Because the stitch pattern is reversible, there is no need to reverse shaping when working the front.

BACK
SLEEVE
Cast on 24 (26, 28) sts.
Work in openwork pat for 4 (4½, 5)"/ 10 (11.5, 12.5)cm, ending with a RS row.

BODY
Next row (WS) Cast on 52 sts, work in openwork pat across— 76 (78, 80) sts. Cont in pat until piece measures 17 (19, 21)"/43 (48, 53.5)cm from body cast-on row, end with a WS row.
Next (gathering) row (RS) *Sl 1 purlwise, k1, psso; rep from * across—38 (39, 40) sts. Bind off.

FRONT
Work as for back.

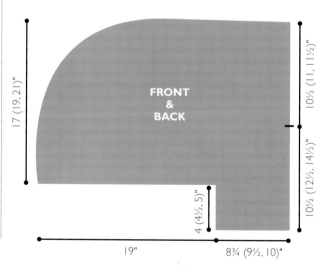

FINISHING

Block pieces to measurements.
Sew side seams. Measure 10½
(12½, 14½)" /26.5 (31.5, 37)cm
in from end of sleeve along top
edge and sew between these
points, leaving rest of top edge
open for neck and shoulder.
Adjust seam length if needed.
Weave in ends. ❤

FRONT
&
BACK

17 (19, 21)"

10½ (11, 11½)"

10½ (12½, 14½)"

4 (4½, 5)"

19"

8¾ (9½, 10)"

▲ The curved front and back create a gathered look when seamed.

Lace hearts cardi

Wear your heart on your sleeve with this classic cardigan. Seed stitch panels alternate with a lacy heart motif on a stockinette stitch background in this feminine fitted charmer.

◼◼◼▶

SIZES
Instructions are written for size X-Small. Changes for Small, Medium, Large, X-Large, and XX-Large are in parentheses. (Shown in size X-Small.)

MEASUREMENTS
BUST (closed) 33 (35, 37, 39, 41, 43)"/84 (89, 94, 99, 104, 109)cm
LENGTH 20½ (21, 21½, 22, 22¼ 22¾)"/52 (53.5, 54.5, 56, 56.5, 58)cm
UPPER ARM 12 (12½, 13, 13¼, 13½, 14)"/30.5 (31.5, 33, 33.5, 34, 35.5)cm

MATERIALS
• 11 (11, 12, 12, 13, 13) 1¾oz/50g balls (each approx 137yd/125m) of Rowan *Pure Wool DK* (wool) in #036 kiss **③**
• One pair each sizes 6 and 7 (4 and 4.5mm) needles *or size to obtain gauge*
• One size 6 (4mm) circular needle, 29"/73cm long
• 7 (7, 7, 7, 8, 8) ⅝"/16mm buttons

GAUGES
22 sts and 34 rows to 4"/10cm over St st using larger needles.
24 sts and 34 rows to 4"/10cm over seed st using larger needles.
➤ Take time to check gauges.

K3, P3 RIB
(over a multiple of 6 sts plus 3)
Row 1 (RS) K3, *p3, k3; rep from * to end.
Row 2 P3, *k3, p3; rep from * to end.
Rep rows 1 and 2 for k3, p3 rib.

SEED STITCH
Work first row over an odd number of sts as foll:
Row 1 (RS) K1, *p1, k1; rep from * across stated number of sts.
Work first row over an even number of sts as foll:
Row 1 (RS) *K1, p1; rep from * across stated number of sts.
Work second row (for odd or even number of sts) as foll:
Row 2 K the purl sts and p the knit sts.
Rep row 2 for seed st.

BACK
With smaller needles, cast on 87 (87, 93, 99, 105, 117) sts. Work in k3, p3 rib for 3"/7.5cm, dec 2 (inc 4, inc 4, inc 4, inc 4, dec 2) sts

MARTIN'S STORY
We are honored that Martin, a star in the international fiber arts community for decades, added his voice to the call for awareness of heart disease, a condition with which he is intimately familiar.

In 2009, Martin's mother suffered a heart attack at the age of 78. Thanks to the advances made in recent years to treating heart disease and the exceptional care provided by the staff and doctors at the local hospital, his mother survived. After experiencing firsthand the fear and helplessness of possibly losing someone he loves as well as the awe at what modern medicine is capable of, the importance of creating awareness of heart disease became abundantly clear to Martin.

A firm believer in managing one's health through diet and exercise, Martin swims at his local pool three to four times a week and walks eight to ten miles every other week in the countryside around his home. Martin pays close attention to what he eats as well. He likes to cook with extra virgin olive oil, keeps fats such as butter and milk to a minimum, avoids sugars whenever possible, and prefers fresh local produce and meats.

evenly spaced across last row and end with a WS row—85 (91, 97, 103, 109, 115) sts. Change to larger needles. Establish seed st and chart 1 as foll:

BEG CHART 1
Row 1 (RS) Work in seed st over first 6 (9, 12, 15, 18, 21) sts, [work chart 1 over next 17 sts, work in seed st over next 11 sts] twice, work chart 1 over next 17 sts, work in seed st over last 6 (9, 12, 15, 18, 21) sts. Keeping sts in seed st as established, cont to foll chart in this way to row 22, then rep rows 1–22 for pat st. AT THE SAME TIME, when piece measures 4½"/11.5cm from beg, ending with a WS row.

SIDE SHAPING
Working new sts in seed st, inc 1 st each side on next row, then every 12th (12th, 12th, 14th, 14th, 14th) row 4 times more—95 (101, 107, 113, 119, 125) sts. Work even until piece measures 12 (12½, 12½, 13, 13, 13½)"/30.5 (31.5, 31.5, 33, 33, 34)cm from beg, ending with a WS row.

ARMHOLE SHAPING
Bind off 5 (6, 6, 7, 7, 8) sts at beg of next 2 rows—85 (89, 95, 99, 105, 109) sts. Dec 1 st each side on next row, then every row 2 (2, 4, 4, 6, 6) times, then every RS row 3 (4, 4, 5, 5, 6) times—73 (75, 77, 79, 81, 83) sts. Work even until armhole measures 7¾ (7¾, 8¼, 8¼, 8½, 8½)"/19.5 (19.5, 21, 21, 21.5, 21.5)cm, end with a WS row.

SHOULDER AND NECK SHAPING
Bind off 7 (7, 7, 7, 7, 8) sts at beg of next 4 rows, then 6 (6, 7, 7, 8, 7) sts at beg of next 2 rows. AT THE SAME TIME, bind off center 25 (27, 27, 29, 29, 29) sts, then bind off from each neck edge 4 sts once.

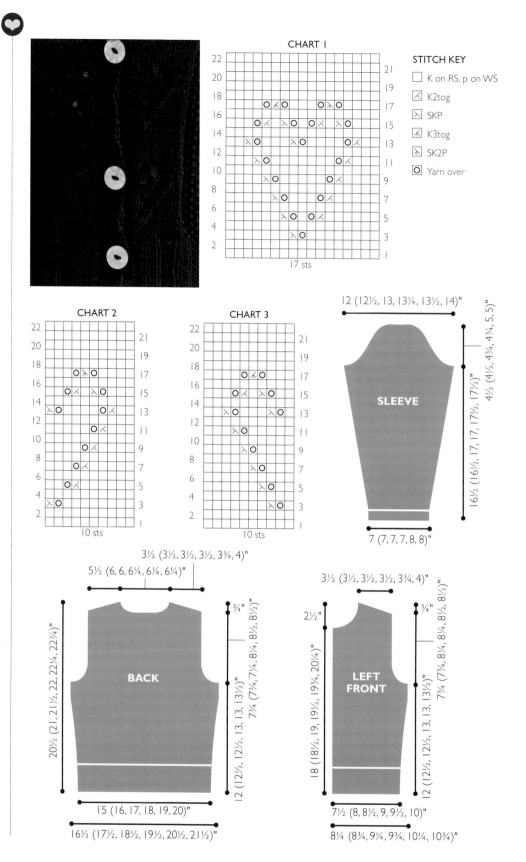

CHART 1

17 sts

STITCH KEY
☐ K on RS, p on WS
◿ K2tog
◺ SKP
◿ K3tog
⋋ SK2P
◯ Yarn over

CHART 2

10 sts

CHART 3

10 sts

12 (12½, 13, 13¼, 13½, 14)"

4½ (4½, 4¾, 4¾, 5, 5)"

SLEEVE

16½ (16½, 17, 17, 17½, 17½)"

7 (7, 7, 7, 8, 8)"

3½ (3½, 3½, 3½, 3¾, 4)"
5½ (6, 6, 6¼, 6¼, 6¼)"
¾"

BACK

20½ (21, 21½, 22, 22¼, 22¾)"

7¾ (7¾, 7¼, 8, 8½, 8½)"

12 (12½, 12½, 13, 13, 13½)"

15 (16, 17, 18, 19, 20)"

16½ (17½, 18½, 19½, 20½, 21½)"

3½ (3½, 3½, 3½, 3¾, 4)"
2½"
¾"

LEFT FRONT

18 (18½, 19, 19½, 19¾, 20¼)"

7¾ (7¾, 8¼, 8¼, 8½, 8½)"

12 (12½, 12½, 13, 13, 13½)"

7½ (8, 8½, 9, 9½, 10)"

8¼ (8¾, 9¼, 9¾, 10¼, 10¾)"

LEFT FRONT

With smaller needles, cast on 45 (45, 51, 51, 57, 57) sts. Work in k3, p3 rib for 3"/7.5cm, dec 1 (inc 2, dec 1, inc 2, dec 1, inc 2) st evenly spaced across last row and end with a WS row—44 (47, 50, 53, 56, 59) sts. Change to larger needles. Establish seed st and charts 1 and 2 as foll:

BEG CHARTS 1 AND 2

Row 1 (RS) Work in seed st over first 6 (9, 12, 15, 18, 21) sts, work chart 1 over next 17 sts, work in seed st over next 11 sts, work chart 2 over last 10 sts. Keeping sts in seed st as established, cont to foll charts in this way to row 22, then rep rows 1–22 for pat st. AT THE SAME TIME, when piece measures 4½"/11.5cm from beg, ending with a WS row.

SIDE SHAPING

Working new sts in seed st, inc 1 st at beg of next row, then at same edge every 12th (12th, 12th, 14th, 14th, 14th) row 4 times more—49 (52, 55, 58, 61, 64) sts. Work even until piece measures same length as back to underarm, end with a WS row.

ARMHOLE SHAPING

Bind off 5 (6, 6, 7, 7, 8) sts at beg of next row—44 (46, 49, 51, 54, 56) sts. Work next row even. Dec 1 st from armhole edge on next row, then every row 2 (2, 4, 4, 6, 6) times, then every RS row 3 (4, 4, 5, 5, 6) times—38 (39, 40, 41, 42, 43) sts. Work even until armhole measures 6 (6, 6½, 6½, 6¾, 6¾)"/15 (15, 16.5, 16.5, 17, 17)cm, ending with a RS row.

NECK SHAPING

At neck edge, bind off 5 (6, 6, 7, 7, 7) sts once, then 5 sts once—28 (28, 29, 29, 30, 31) sts. Dec 1 st from neck edge on next row, then every row 3 times more, then every RS row 4 times—20 (20, 21, 21, 22, 23) sts. Work even until piece measures same length as back to shoulder, ending with a WS row.

SHOULDER SHAPING

At armhole edge, bind off 7 (7, 7, 7, 7, 8) sts twice, then 6 (6, 7, 7, 8, 7) sts once.

RIGHT FRONT

With smaller needles, cast on 45 (45, 51, 51, 57, 57) sts. Work in k3, p3 rib for 3"/7.5cm, dec 1 (inc 2, dec 1, inc 2, dec 1, inc 2) st evenly spaced across last row and end with a WS row—44 (47, 50, 53, 56, 59) sts. Change to larger needles. Establish seed st and charts 3 and 1 as foll:

BEG CHARTS 3 AND 1

Row 1 (RS) Work chart 3 over first 10 sts, work in seed st over next 11 sts, work chart 1 over next 17 sts, work in seed st over last 6 (9, 12, 15, 18, 21) sts. Keeping sts in seed st as established, cont to foll charts in this way to row 22, then rep

rows 1–22 for pat st. AT THE SAME TIME, when piece measures 4½"/11.5cm from beg, end with a WS row. Cont to work same as left front, reversing all shaping.

SLEEVES

With smaller needles, cast on 51 (51, 51, 51, 57, 57) sts. Work in k3, p3 rib for 1"/2.5cm, inc 0 (0, 2, 2, 0, 0) sts evenly spaced across last row and end with a WS row—51 (51, 53, 53, 57, 57) sts. Change to larger needles. Establish seed st and chart 1 as foll:

BEG CHART 1

Row 1 (RS) Work in seed st over first 17 (17, 18, 18, 20, 20) sts, work chart 1 over center 17 sts, work seed st over last 17 (17, 18, 18, 20, 20) sts. Keeping sts in seed st as established, cont to foll chart in this way to row 22, then rep rows 1–22 for pat st. AT THE SAME TIME, when piece measures 2"/5cm from beg, end with a WS row. Working new sts in seed st, inc 1 st each side on next row, then every 8th row 0 (2, 0, 5, 0, 3) times, every 10th row 7 (9, 11, 7, 9, 9) times, then every 12th row 3 (0, 0, 0, 2, 0) times—73 (75, 77, 79, 81, 83) sts. Work even until piece measures 16½ (16½, 17, 17, 17½, 17½)"/42 (42, 43, 43, 44.5, 44.5)cm from beg, ending with a WS row.

CAP SHAPING

Bind off 5 (6, 6, 7, 7, 8) sts at beg of next 2 rows—63 (63, 65, 65, 67, 67) sts. Dec 1 st each side on next row, then *every* row twice, every RS row 6 (6, 7, 7, 8, 8) times, every 4th row twice, every RS row 5 times, then *every* row 4 times. Bind off rem 23 sts.

FINISHING

Block pieces to measurements. Sew shoulder seams.

NECKBAND

With RS facing and smaller needles, pick up and k 25 (27, 27, 29, 29, 29) sts evenly spaced along right front neck edge, 33 (35, 35, 37, 37, 37) sts along back neck edge, then 25 (27, 27, 29, 29, 29) sts along left front neck edge—83 (89, 89, 95, 95, 95) sts. Cont in rib as foll:
Rows 1 and 3 (WS) K1, p3, *k3, p3; rep from * to last st, end k1.
Rows 2 and 4 K4, *p3, k3; rep from * to last st, end k1.
Row 5 Rep row 1. Bind off in rib.

BUTTON BAND

With RS facing and circular needle, pick up and k 101 (101, 107, 107, 113, 113) sts evenly spaced along entire left front edge. Rep rows 1–5 same as for neckband. Bind off in rib. Place markers for 7 (7, 7, 7, 8, 8) buttonholes along right front edge, with the first ½"/1.5cm from lower edge, the last ½"/1.5cm from top edge and the other 5 (5, 5, 5, 6, 6) evenly spaced between.

BUTTONHOLE BAND

With RS facing and circular needle, pick up and k 101 (101, 107, 107, 113, 113) sts evenly spaced along entire right front edge. Rep rows 1–3 same as neckband.
Row (buttonhole) 4 (RS) *Work in rib to marker, work next 2 sts tog, yo; rep from * 6 (6, 6, 6, 7, 7) times more; work in rib to end. Rep row 5. Bind off in rib.
Set in sleeves.
Sew side and sleeve seams.
Sew on buttons. ♥

Cowl-neck Vest

This sporty short-sleeve cardigan is ideal for layering. Wear it over long sleeves for an autumn stroll or walk to the gym, or under a coat on colder days—no scarf required!

CECILY'S STORY
We were lucky enough to collaborate with Winged Knits designer Cecily Glowick MacDonald on our catalog "The Hand-Dyed Issue." It was a great experience for all, and Cecily leapt at the chance to work with us again on *Knit Red.* Like any passionate knitter, Cecily wants to knit as long and as much as possible, and is thankful to be able to bring awareness of heart disease to knitters around the globe. Cecily always takes the time to get plenty of exercise and watch what she eats. A resident of Portland, Maine, Cecily takes full advantage of her surroundings. During the summers you will find her taking a stroll along the beach or a swim in the ocean. The rest of the year she keeps her promenades in town, exploring the streets of her lovely city!

SIZES
Instructions are written for size Small. Changes for Medium and Large are in parentheses. (Shown in size Small.)

MEASUREMENTS
BUST 33½ (36½, 39½)"/85 (92.5, 100)cm
LENGTH 22½ (24, 25½)"/57 (61, 65)cm

MATERIALS
• 6 (7, 8) 3½ oz/100g balls (each approx 138yd/126m) of Manos Del Uruguay *Wool Clasica* (wool) in #48 cherry (4)
• Size 9 (5.5mm) circular needle 29"/75cm long, *or size to obtain gauge*
• One set (5) size 9 double-pointed needles (dpns)
• Size 10 (6mm) circular needle, 29"/75cm long
• Stitch markers
• Stitch holders or waste yarn
• Ten ⅞"/22mm buttons

GAUGE
15 sts and 21 rows to 4"/10cm over St st using smaller needles.
➤ Take time to check gauge.

CECILY'S TIP
CECILY AND HER HUSBAND HAVE A ONE-CAR HOUSEHOLD, so when she is without wheels, Cecily likes to do errands on foot. This is a great way to get some exercise while getting things done. Maximize your workout by adding a block or two to your route and carrying your own groceries!

STITCH GLOSSARY
K1-r/b Slightly twist work on LH needle toward you so that WS of work is visible. Insert RH needle from top down into next st on LH needle one row below. Knit this st, then knit st on LH needle (1 st increased).

BACKWARD LOOP CAST-ON
*Wrap yarn around left thumb from front to back and secure in palm. Insert needle upward through strand on thumb. Slip loop from thumb onto RH needle, pulling yarn to tighten;

rep from * for desired number of sts.

NOTE
Vest is worked from the top down in one piece.

VEST
COWL
With larger needle, cast on 102 sts. Work in garter st for 3 rows. Then work in St st until piece measures 13½"/34.5cm from beg, ending with a WS row.
Next row (RS) K7, *k1, k2tog; rep from * to last 8 sts, k8—73 sts.

YOKE
Change to smaller needle.
Next row P13, pm, p9, pm, p29, pm, p9, pm, p13.
Next (inc) row (RS) *Work to 2 sts before marker, k1-r/b, k1, sl marker, k1, k1-r/b; rep from * 3 times more, knit to end—8 sts inc. Rep inc row every other row 9 (12, 15) times more, then every

4th row 4 times—185 (209, 233) sts. Yoke measures 7 (8, 9)"/18 (20.5, 23)cm, ending with a WS row.

DIVIDE SLEEVES AND BODY
Next row (RS) K 27 (30, 33) sts for left front, remove marker, place next 37 (43, 49) sts on holder for left sleeve, remove marker, using the backward loop cast-on, cast on 3 sts at underarm, pm for side, cast on 3 more sts, knit across 57 (63, 69) sts for back, remove marker, place next 37 (43, 49) sts on holder for right sleeve, remove marker, cast on 3 sts at underarm, pm for side, cast on 3 more sts, knit to end for right front—123 (135, 147) sts.

BODY
Work even in St st until piece measures 2"/5cm from under-arms, ending with a WS row.
Next (dec) row (RS) *Work to 3 sts before side marker, ssk, k1, sl marker, k1, k2tog; rep from * once more—4 sts dec. Rep dec row every 6th row once, then every 8th row twice—107 (119, 131) sts. Work even in St st until piece measures 8½ (8½, 9)"/21.5 (21.5, 23)cm from underarm, end with a WS row.
Next (inc) row (RS) *Work to 2 sts before marker, k1-r/b, k1, sl marker, k1, k1-r/b; rep from * once more—4 sts inc. Rep inc row every 4th row once, then every 6th row 3 times—127 (139, 151) sts. Work even in St st until piece measures 14½ (15, 15½)"/37 (38, 39.5)cm from underarm, end with a RS row. Work in garter st for 5 rows. Bind off loosely.

SLEEVES
Place 37 (43, 49) sleeve sts on dpns. Join yarn and pick up and k 3 sts in underarm cast-on, pm, pick up and k 3 more sts in underarm cast-on, knit to end—43 (49, 55) sts. Join and work in garter st for 3 rnds (k 1 rnd, p 1 rnd). Bind off loosely.

FINISHING
Block pieces to measurements.

BUTTONHOLE BAND
With smaller needle, pick up and k 152 (156,160) sts along right front and edge of cowl. Work in garter st for 3 rows.
Next row (RS) K4 (6, 8), [k2tog, yo, k14] 9 times, k2tog, yo, k2 (4, 6). Work in garter st for 2 rows. Bind off.

BUTTON BAND
With smaller needle, pick up and k 152 (156,160) sts along left front and edge of cowl. Work in garter st for 6 rows. Bind off.

POCKETS
(MAKE 2, OPTIONAL)
With smaller needle, cast on 20 sts. Purl 1 row.
Next row (RS) Knit.
Next row K2, purl to last 2 sts, k2. Rep last 2 rows until piece measures 4¼"/11cm, ending with a RS row. Work in garter st for 3 rows. Bind off.
Sew pockets to body, 1"/2.5cm from lower edge and 1¾"/4.5cm in from front edge. Sew buttons opposite buttonholes. ❤

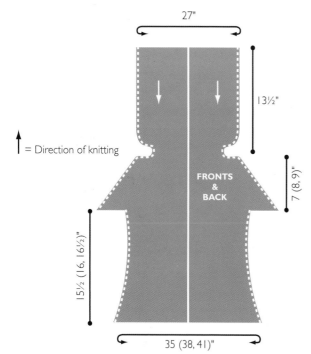

27"

↑ = Direction of knitting

13½"

7 (8, 9)"

FRONTS & BACK

15½ (16, 16½)"

35 (38, 41)"

33½ (36½, 39½)"

Snowboarder hat

Even if winter sports aren't your thing, you'll love knitting and wearing this cozy hat, created by Lindsey Jacobellis and the Red Heart Design Team.

SIZES
Instructions are written for Small/Medium. Changes for Large/X-Large are in parentheses. (Shown in size Small/Medium.)

MEASUREMENTS
CIRCUMFERENCE
20 (22)"/51 (56)cm
DEPTH 8½"/21.5cm
(excluding earflaps)

MATERIALS
• 2 3½oz/100g balls (each approx 183yd/167m) of Stitch Nation *Washable Ewe* (superwash wool) in #3903 strawberry (4)
• One pair size 10 (6mm) needles *or size to obtain gauge*
• Two size 10 (6mm) double-pointed needles (dpns) for I-cords
• Stitch holders
• Stitch markers

GAUGE
14 sts and 28 rows to 4"/10cm over garter st using 2 strands held tog and size 10 (6mm) needles.
➤Take time to check gauge.

NOTE
Use 2 strands of yarn held tog throughout.

EARFLAPS (MAKE 2)
I-CORD TIE
With dpn and 2 strands held tog, cast on 3 sts, leaving a long tail for sewing. Work I-cord as foll:
*Next row (RS) With 2nd dpn, k3, do not turn. Slide sts back to beg of needle to work next row from RS; rep from * until I-cord measures 7½ (8½)"/19 (21.5)cm from beg. Change to straight needles.

EARFLAP
Cont to work back and forth in garter st (knit every row) as foll:
Inc row 1 (RS) K1, M1, k1, M1, k1—5 sts. Knit next row.
Inc row 2 (RS) K1, M1, knit to last st, end M1, k1—7 sts. Knit next row. Rep last 2 rows 5 (6) times more, ending with a WS row—17 (19) sts. Place sts on holder.

HAT
With straight needles and 2 strands of yarn held tog, cast on 9 (10) sts, k 17 (19) sts from first earflap holder, cast on 20 (21) sts, k 17 (19) sts from 2nd earflap holder, then cast on 9 (10) sts—72 (79) sts. Cont in garter st for 5 rows, dec 1 (2) sts evenly spaced across last row and end with a WS row—71 (77) sts. Cont in large checked pat st as foll:
Row 1 (RS) K1 (selvage st), knit to last st, pm, k1 (selvage st).
Row 2 P1, sl marker, knit to next marker, sl marker, p1.
Row 3 Knit, slipping markers.
Row 4 P1, sl marker, p3, *k3, p3; rep from *, end sl marker, p1.
Row 5 Rep row 3.
Row 6 Rep row 4.
Rows 7 and 9 Rep row 3.
Rows 8 and 10 Rep row 2.
Row 11 Rep row 3.
Row 12 P1, sl marker, k3, *p3, k3; rep from *, end sl marker, p1.
Row 13 Rep row 3.
Row 14 Rep row 12.
Row 15 Rep row 3.
Row (inc) 16 (WS) K1, sl marker, knit to next marker, inc 10 sts evenly spaced, end sl marker, k1—81 (87) sts. Cont in small checked pat st as foll:
Row 1 (RS) K1, sl marker, *k1, p2; rep from * to last 2 sts, end k1, sl marker, k1.

▲ Earflaps and I-cord ties are both practical and a fun design element.

♥**LINDSEY'S TIP**
CHALLENGE YOURSELF!
Avoid getting in a rut or
stepping back into bad
habits by giving yourself a
reason to stay healthy.
Whether you decide to
train for a community 5K
run/walk or switch to a
vegetarian diet, setting goals
is a great way to get
motivated and stay healthy!

Row 2 P1, sl marker, p1, *k2, p1;
rep from *, end sl marker,
p1 to end.
Row 3 Knit, slipping markers.
Row 4 P1, slipping markers. Rep
rows 1–4 twice more.
Next (dec) row (RS) K1, sl
marker, knit to next marker, dec 9
(8) sts evenly spaced, end sl
marker, k1—72 (79) sts. Keeping
1 st each side in St st (knit on RS,
purl on WS) for selvage sts, cont
to work even in garter st over
rem sts for 3 rows.

CROWN SHAPING
Dec row 1 (RS) K1, sl marker, *k5,
k2tog; rep from * to last st, end sl
marker, k1—62 (68) sts.
Next row P1, sl marker, knit to
next marker, sl marker, p1.
Dec row 2 K1, sl marker, *k4,
k2tog; rep from * to last st, end sl
marker, k1—52 (57) sts.
Next row P1, sl marker, knit to
next marker, sl marker, p1.
Dec row 3 K1, sl marker, *k3,
k2tog; rep from * to last st, end sl
marker, k1—42 (46) sts.
Next row P1, sl marker, knit to
next marker, sl marker, p1.
Dec row 4 K1, sl marker, *k2,
k2tog; rep from * to last st, end sl
marker, k1—32 (35) sts.
Next row P1, sl marker, knit to
next marker, sl marker, p1.

Dec row 5 K1, sl marker, *k1,
k2tog; rep from * to last st, end sl
marker, k1—22 (24) sts.
Next row P1, sl marker, knit to
next marker, sl marker, p1.
Dec row 6 K1, sl marker, *k2tog;
rep from * to last st, end sl
marker, k1—12 (13) sts.
Next row P1, drop marker, knit to
next marker, drop marker, p1.
Dec row 7 K 0 (1), *k2tog; rep
from * to end—6 (7) sts.
Next row Knit.
Dec row 8 [K2tog] 3 times, end
k 0 (1)—3 (4) sts.
Next row Knit across, dec 0 (1) st
at end of row—3 sts. Change to
dpns. Cont in I-cord for 1"/2.5cm.
Cut yarn, leaving an 8"/20.5cm
tail. Thread tail into tapestry
needle, then thread through rem
sts. Pull tog tightly, secure end,
then weave in end.

FINISHING
Sew back seam. For each earflap
I-cord tie, thread beg tail into
tapestry needle, then sew
running stitches around open
edge. Pull tog tightly to close
opening, then secure and
weave in end.♥

♥ **IRIS SCHREIER**

Silk and mohair cape

Luxurious yarns sparkling with metallic threads and glass beads create a glamorous, evening-ready cover-up. The cabled edging, which adds a sumptuous touch, is attached as you knit it.

◀■■■▶

SIZE
Instructions are written for one size.

MEASUREMENTS
Approx 40"/101.5cm wide × 30"/76cm long

MATERIALS
• 2 2¾oz/80g hanks (each approx 400yd/366m) of Artyarns *Rhapsody Glitter Light* (silk/mohair/metallic) in #2244 red with silver glitter (MC) (**4**)
• 2 1¾oz/50g hanks (each approx 165yd/151m) of Artyarns *Mohair Splash* (silk/mohair/glass beads) in #244 red with beads (CC) (**4**)
• Two size 10½ (6.5mm) circular needles, 32"/80cm long, *or size to obtain gauge*
• One pair size 10 (6mm) needles
• Cable needle (cn)
• Stitch markers
• One ⅞" × 1⅝"/22mm × 41mm sweater clasp

GAUGE
12 sts and 21 rows to 4"/10cm over pat st using size 10½ (6.5mm) circular needle.
➤ Take time to check gauge.

NOTE
Cable trim is added after cape is completed. It is attached to edge of cape as you knit the trim.

STITCH GLOSSARY
12-st LC Sl 6 sts to cn and hold to front, k6, k6 from cn.
kf&b Inc 1 by knitting into the front and back of the next st.

CAPE
BOTTOM POINT
With circular needle and MC, cast on 3 sts.
Setup row (WS) K1, kf&b, pm,

k1—4 sts.
Row 1 (RS) Kf&b, knit to marker, drop marker, kf&b, pm, knit to end—6 sts.
Rows 2–6 Rep row 1—16 sts.
Row 7 K2tog, knit to marker, drop marker, kf&b, pm, knit to end—16 sts.
Row 8 P2tog, purl to marker, drop marker, kf&b, pm, purl to end—16 sts. Rep rows 1–8 eight times more, then rows 1–6 once—124 sts. With RS facing, leave first 62 sts on working needle for upper right half of heart, then place rem 62 sts on

IRIS'S STORY
We have had the pleasure of working with Iris, founder and head designer of Artyarns, for many years, and it seemed only natural to have her on board for *Knit Red*. She's an exceptional designer—not to mention the creator of some of the most exquisite handpainted yarns we've ever seen—and we were so excited to see what she would dream up! Heart disease hits close to home for Iris. Her father-in-law, uncle, and cousin have all endured bypass surgery, and her mother-in-law has suffered multiple heart attacks. Three years ago, Iris made a commitment to improve her quality of life by avoiding processed foods, refined sugars, white flour, and corn syrup. By focusing on eating meals that include lean proteins, organic fruits and vegetables, and whole grains and taking holistic supplements daily, Iris says she has been able to drastically reduce her cravings for sweets, maintain her body weight, build muscles, and increase her strength. She also has tons of energy! Of course, change doesn't come easily, so Iris enlisted the help of a nutritionist to get her on the right track.

♥ **IRIS'S TIP**
VARIETY IS THE SPICE OF LIFE!
If you tend to bore easily in your exercise habits, consider doing something different every day or every other day of the week. Iris lifts weights and does some form of cardio activity three times a week (not necessarily on the same days) and takes a yoga class. By rotating activities you can work different areas of the body as well as keep your exercise routine fun and interesting!

last 2 sts, k2tog—58 sts.
Rows 3 and 4 With MC, rep row 2—54 sts.
Rows 5 and 6 With CC, rep row 2—50 sts.
Row 7 With MC, rep row 2—48 sts.
Row 8 With MC, purl to marker; drop marker, p2tog, pm, purl to last 2 sts, p2tog—46 sts.
Rows 9 and 10 With CC, rep row 2—42 sts.
Rows 11 and 12 With MC, rep row 2—38 sts.
Rows 13 and 14 With CC, rep row 2—34 sts.
Rows 15 With MC, rep row 2—32 sts.
Row 16 With MC, purl to marker; drop marker, p2tog, pm, purl to last 2 sts, p2tog—30 sts. Rep rows 9–16 once more, then rows 9–13 once—4 sts. Bind off.

UPPER LEFT HALF OF HEART
With RS facing, join MC and cont on 2nd needle as foll:
Row 1 (RS) Kf&b, knit to last 2 sts, k2tog—62 sts.
Row 2 Purl.
Rows 3–8 Knit. Rep rows 1–8 four times more, then rows 1 and 2 once—62 sts.

FILL IN
Row 1 (RS) With CC, k2tog, k30, pm, k2tog, k28—60 sts.
Row 2 With CC, k2tog, knit to marker; drop marker, k2tog, pm, knit to end—58 sts.
Rows 3 and 4 With MC, rep row 2—54 sts.
Rows 5 and 6 With CC, rep row 2—50 sts.
Row 7 With MC, rep row 2—48 sts.
Row 8 With MC, p2tog, purl to marker; drop marker, p2tog, pm, purl to end—46 sts.
Rows 9 and 10 With CC, rep row 2—42 sts.
Rows 11 and 12 With MC, rep row 2—38 sts.
Rows 13 and 14 With CC, rep row 2—34 sts.
Rows 15 With MC, rep row 2—32 sts.
Row 16 With MC, p2tog, purl to marker; drop marker, p2tog, pm, purl to end—30 sts.
Rep rows 9–16 once more, then rows 9–13 once—4 sts. Bind off.

CABLE TRIM
With straight needles and CC, cast on 13 sts. With RS facing, beg in side edge of center of bottom point.
Row 1 (RS) K12, sl last st, pick up and k 1 st at side edge of cape, pass slip st over; turn.
Row 2 P13.
Rows 3 and 5 Rep row 1.
Rows 4 and 6 Rep row 2.
Row 7 12-st LC, sl last st, pick up and k 1 st in side edge of cape, pass slip st over; turn.
Row 8 Rep row 2.
Rows 9, 11, and 13 Rep row 1.
Rows 10, 12, and 14 Rep row 2.
Rep rows 1–14 for cable pat. Cont to work in this way around entire edge of cape, ending at bottom point. Bind off.

FINISHING
Sew cast-on and bind-off edges of cable trim tog. Sew on clasp. ♥

2nd circular needle for upper left half of heart.

UPPER RIGHT HALF OF HEART
With working needle, cont as foll:
Row 1 (RS) K2tog, knit to last st, kf&b—62 sts. **Row 2** Purl.
Rows 3–8 Knit. Rep rows 1–8

four times more, then rows 1 and 2 once—62 sts.

FILL IN
Row 1 (RS) With CC, k28, k2tog, pm, k30, k2tog—60 sts.
Row 2 With CC, knit to marker; drop marker, k2tog, pm, knit to

Heart motif mitts

A pretty lace heart pattern runs the length of these fingerless mitts. Knit in Debbie's new washable yarn, these cozy handwarmers make a quick and handy gift.

■■■□

SIZE
Instructions are written for one size.

MEASUREMENTS
HAND CIRCUMFERENCE
7½"/19cm (unstretched)
LENGTH
Approx 12½"/31.5cm

MATERIALS
• 1 3½oz/100g ball (each approx 183yd/167m) of Stitch Nation by Debbie Stoller *Washable Ewe* (wool) in #3903 strawberry (4)
• One pair each sizes 5 and 6 (3.75 and 4mm) needles *or size to obtain gauge*
• One set (4) size 6 (4mm) double-pointed needles (dpns)
• Stitch markers

GAUGE
20 sts and 27 rows to 4"/10cm over St st using larger needles.
➤ Take time to check gauge.

NOTES
1) Mitts are worked back and forth on two needles.
2) Thumbs are worked back and forth on 3 dpns.

K2, P2 RIB
(over multiple of 4 sts plus 2)
Row 1 (RS) K2, *p2, k2; rep from * to end.
Row 2 P2, *k2, p2; rep from * to end.
Rep rows 1 and 2 for k2, p2 rib.

LEFT MITT
With larger needles, cast on 38 sts. Work in k2, p2 rib for 10 rows, dec 1 st at end of last row and end with a WS row—37 sts.

BEG CHART PAT
Row 1 (RS) K18, pm, k1 (thumb gusset), pm, k2, work chart pat over next 13 sts, k3.
Row 2 P3, work chart pat over next 13 sts, p2, sl marker, p1, sl marker, p18. Cont to foll chart in this way to row 15, then rep rows 6–15 three times more, then rows 6–10 once, ending with a WS row.

THUMB GUSSET
Next row (RS) Knit to first marker, sl marker, M1, k1, M1, sl marker, k2, work chart row 11 over next 13 sts, k3—39 sts. Cont to inc 1 st after first marker and 1 st before 2nd marker every other row 5 times more—49 sts. AT THE SAME TIME, cont to foll chart to row 15, then rep rows 6–11 once, ending

with a RS row.
Next row (WS) P3, work chart row 12 over next 13 sts, p2, drop marker, place next 13 sts on scrap yarn for thumb, drop marker, cast on 1 st, p18—37 sts. Working as established, cont to work chart to row 15, then rep rows 6–15 once more, ending with a RS row. Change to smaller needles.
Next row (WS) Purl across, dec 1 st at end—36 sts. Work in k2, p2 rib for 4 rows. Bind off in rib.

THUMB
Place 13 sts on scrap yarn on 3 dpns (5 sts on first needle and 4 sts on 2nd and 3rd needles). Join yarn, then with 4th needle, k13, then pick up and k 1 st in cast-on st at base of thumb—14 sts (5 sts on first needle, 4 sts on 2nd needle, and 5 sts on 3rd needle). Working back and forth, purl next row. Cont in k2, p2 rib for 4 rows. Bind off in rib.

RIGHT MITT
With larger needles, cast on 38 sts. Work in k2, p2 rib for 10 rows, dec 1 st at end of last row and end with a WS row—37 sts.

BEG CHART PAT
Row 1 (RS) K3, work chart pat over next 13 sts, k2, pm, k1 (thumb gusset), pm, k18.
Row 2 P18, sl marker, p1, sl marker, p2, work chart pat over next 13 sts, p3. Cont to foll chart

DEBBIE'S STORY
We couldn't be happier to enlist the creative energies of Debbie Stoller, author of the famed Stitch 'N Bitch series and co-founder of *Bust* magazine, as part of *Knit Red*. Recently, Debbie's favorite aunt, who helped nurture her crafty talents, was diagnosed with a small heart attack. Her aunt had no idea at the time that what she was experiencing was actually a heart attack. Thankfully, she's doing well, but the incident reinforced for Debbie how important it is to stay informed about the symptoms of heart disease. Debbie's philosophy for living a heart-healthy life revolves around stress reduction and taking the time to really appreciate the world around her. She takes long walks to bird-watch and admire the old houses in her Brooklyn neighborhood, which keeps her fit and helps her to clear her mind and reduce stress.

❤**DEBBIE'S TIP**
TRY SOMETHING NEW!
Debbie loves vegetables, and
when she goes to the
farmers' market she seeks
out a veggie she's never
heard of (ramps, garlic
scapes, avocado squash, etc.),
then learns how to cook it.
This strategy will keep
you from falling into a
culinary rut, and you might
just discover your new
favorite dish!

in this way to row 15, then rep
rows 6–15 three times more,
then rows 6–10 once, ending
with a WS row.

THUMB GUSSET
Next row (RS) K3, work chart
row 11 over next 13 sts, k2, sl
marker, M1, k1, M1, sl marker,
k18—39 sts. Cont to inc 1 st
after first marker and 1 st before
2nd marker every other row 5
times more—49 sts. AT THE
SAME TIME, cont to foll chart to
row 15, then rep rows 6–11
once, end with a RS row.
Next row (WS) P18, drop
marker, place next 13 sts on
scrap yarn for thumb, drop
marker, cast on 1 st, p2, work
chart row 12 over next 13 sts,
p3—37 sts. Working as
established, cont to work chart
to row 15, then rep rows 6–15
once more, ending with a RS row.
Change to smaller needles.
Next row (WS) Purl across,
dec 1 st at end—36 sts. Work in
k2, p2 rib for 4 rows.
Bind off in rib.

THUMB
Work as for left mitt.

FINISHING
Sew side and thumb seams. Block
pieces to measurements.❤

STITCH KEY

☐	K on RS, p on WS
⟍	K2tog
⟋	Ssk
⅄	SK2P
⋀	S2KP
◯	Yarn over

13 sts

AMY SWENSON

Eyelet shawl

This feminine wrap sets the stage for romance. Wear it as a light cover-up in summer or over an evening dress any time.

■■■▭

SIZE
Instructions are written for one size.

MEASUREMENTS
Approx 52"/132cm wide × 21½"/54.5cm long

MATERIALS
• 1 3½oz/100g hanks (each approx 275yd/252m) of Lorna's Laces *Honor* (baby alpaca/silk) in bold red (**3**)
• Size 7 (4.5mm) circular needle, 32"/81cm long *or size to obtain gauge*
• Stitch markers

GAUGE
13 sts and 20 rows to 4"/10cm over St st using size 7 (4.5mm) circular needle (after blocking).
➤ Take time to check gauge.

NOTE
Shawl is worked from the top down.

AMY'S STORY
Amy, the creative genius behind the stylish Indigirl pattern label, first encountered heart disease at an early age. When she was just 10 years old, her father had quintuple bypass surgery to fix severe blockages in his heart. Her family's lives changed almost overnight: Skim milk and chicken replaced cream and ground beef. Thankfully, the surgery was a success, and even though her dad was 68 at the time, he went on to enjoy many more years of healthy eating before he passed away at the age of 90 due to a stroke. Amy is grateful not only to the surgeons and doctors who prevented a heart attack, but to her father for making healthy choices that allowed him to enjoy another two decades with his family. About two years ago Amy decided to change her diet and exercise habits and lost 40 pounds! She began walking to work (about a three-mile trek each way), which she finds not only keeps her in shape but allows her to start and end the day in a great mood.

AMY'S TIP
AVOID TEMPTATION! By investing in a desktop coffeemaker instead of visiting the coffee shop in the lobby of the building where she works, Amy steers clear of sweet treats like muffins and doughnuts.

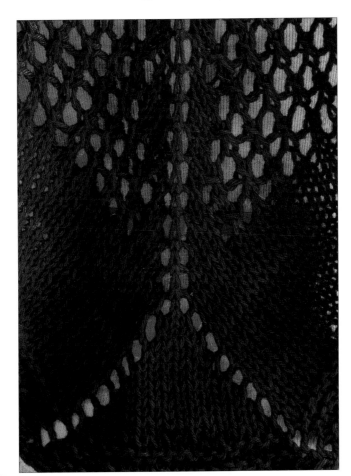

SHAWL
Beg at top edge, cast on 7 sts.
Next row (WS) Knit.

BEG CHART PATS
Row 1 (RS) K2 (right edging chart), pm, yo, k1, yo (right half chart) pm, k1 (center st chart), pm, yo, k1, yo (left half chart), pm, k2 (left edging chart)—11 sts.
Row 2 K2 (left edging chart), sl marker, purl to next marker (left half chart), sl marker, p1 (center st chart), sl marker, purl to next marker (right half chart), sl marker, k2 (right edging chart). Cont to foll charts in this way to row 22, end with a WS row—51 sts. To cont, rep rows 15–22 (8-row rep) of charts 7 times more as foll:
First 8-row rep Work 4-st rep on right half and left half charts twice—67 sts.

Second 8-row rep Work 4-st rep on right half and left half charts 3 times—83 sts.

Third 8-row rep Work 4-st rep on right half and left half charts 4 times—99 sts.

Fourth 8-row rep Work 4-st rep on right half and left half charts 5 times—115 sts.

Fifth 8-row rep Work 4-st rep on right half and left half charts 6 times—131 sts.

Sixth 8-row rep Work 4-st rep on right half and left half charts 7 times—147 sts.

Seventh 8-row rep Work 4-st rep on right half and left half charts 8 times—163 sts.

TOP EDGING

Set-up row (RS) K2, yo, sl marker, knit to next marker, sl marker, yo, k1 (center st), yo, sl marker, knit to next marker, sl marker, yo, k2—167 sts.

Next row (WS) K2, [purl to marker, sl marker] 3 times, purl to last 2 sts, k2.

Next row (RS) K2, knit to next marker, yo, sl marker, knit to next marker, sl marker, yo, knit to next marker, yo, sl marker, knit to next marker, sl marker, yo, knit to end—171 sts. Rep last 2 rows 6 times more, end with a RS row—195 sts.

Cont in garter st as foll:

Next row (WS) Knit to 1 st before marker, p1, sl marker, knit to next marker, sl marker, p1, knit to 1 st before next marker, p1, sl marker, knit to next marker, sl marker, p1, knit to end.

Next row (RS) K2, knit to next marker, yo, sl marker, knit to next marker, sl marker, yo, knit to next marker, yo, sl marker, knit to next marker, sl marker, yo, k to end—199 sts. Rep last 2 rows 3 times more, then work one WS row more—211 sts. Bind off all sts loosely knitwise.

FINISHING

Block piece to measurements. ❤

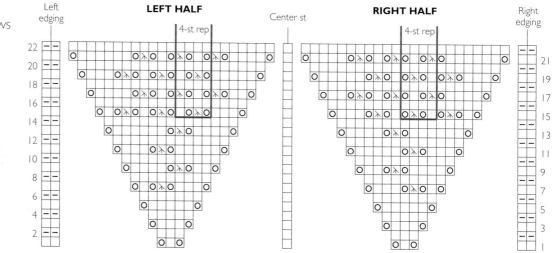

STITCH KEY

☐ K on RS, p on WS

⊟ K on WS

⃗ SK2P

◯ Yarn over

LEFT HALF   Center st   **RIGHT HALF**

Left edging   4-st rep   4-st rep   Right edging

SARAH HATTON

Mohair twist sweater

Channel your inner ballerina when you wear this graceful top.
The front is a rectangle that is twisted before seaming.

SIZES
Instructions are written for size
Small. Changes for Medium, Large,
and X-Large are in parentheses.
Shown in size Small.

MEASUREMENTS
BUST 35 (39, 44, 49)"/89
(99, 111.5, 124.5)cm
LENGTH 16 (16½, 17½,
18)"/40.5 (42, 44.5, 45.5)cm
UPPER ARM 15 (16, 17, 18)"/38
(40.5, 43, 45.5)cm

MATERIALS
• 4 (4, 5, 5) .88oz/25g balls
(each approx 229yd/210m) of
Rowan *Kidsilk Haze* (super kid
mohair/silk) in #627 blood

• One pair size 6 (4mm) needles
or size to obtain gauge

• One size 6 (4mm) circular
needle, 29"/73cm long

GAUGE
22 sts and 31 rows to
4"/10cm over St st using
size 6 (4mm) needles.
➤ Take time to check your gauge.

BACK
With straight needles, cast on
97 (107, 121, 135) sts. Knit next 2
rows. Cont in St st (knit on RS,
purl on WS) until piece measures
16 (16½, 17½, 18)"/40.5 (42,
44.5, 45.5)cm from beg, ending
with a WS row. Knit next 2 rows.
Bind off knitwise.

FRONT
With circular needle, cast on 139
(153, 173, 193) sts. Knit next 2
rows. Cont in St st (knit on RS,
purl on WS) until piece measures
same length as back to shoulder,
end with a WS row. Knit next 2
rows. Bind off knitwise.

SLEEVES
With straight needles, cast on 61
(61, 67, 67) sts. Knit next 2 rows.

Cont in St st and work even until
piece measures 9"/23cm from
beg, ending with a WS row.
Inc row (RS) K1, M1, knit to last
st, M1, k1. Rep inc row every 4th
row 3 (10, 5, 15) times more,
then every 6th row 7 (3, 7, 0)
times—83 (89, 93, 99) sts.
Work even until piece measures
18 (18½, 19, 19)"/45.5 (47, 48,
48)cm, ending with a WS row.
Bind off knitwise.

FINISHING
Sew a 3 (4, 5, 6¼)"/7.5 (10, 12.5,
16)cm right shoulder seam.
Place back/front on work surface
so RS of front is facing up and
right shoulder seam is at top
right. Twist front piece twice so
RS (knit side) is again facing up.
Sew a 3 (4, 5, 6¼)"/7.5 (10, 12.5,
16)cm left shoulder seam.
Place markers 7½ (8, 8½, 9)"/19
(20.5, 21.5, 23)cm down from
shoulders on back and front.
Sew sleeves to armholes
between markers. Sew side and
sleeve seams. ❤

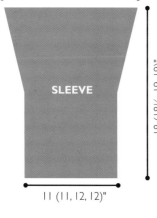

SLEEVE

15 (16, 17, 18)"

18 (18½, 19, 19)"

11 (11, 12, 12)"

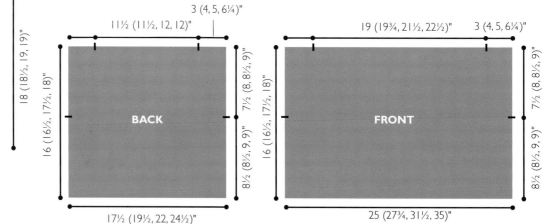

BACK

11½ (11½, 12, 12)"

3 (4, 5, 6¼)"

16 (16½, 17½, 18)"

7½ (8, 8½, 9)"

8½ (8½, 9, 9)"

17½ (19½, 22, 24½)"

FRONT

19 (19¾, 21½, 22½)"

3 (4, 5, 6¼)"

16 (16½, 17½, 18)"

7½ (8, 8½, 9)"

8½ (8½, 9, 9)"

25 (27¾, 31½, 35)"

♥ MAIE LANDRA

Modular dress

You'll be the center of attention in this showstopper. Maie's signature modular construction highlights the two shades of red.

▪▪▪▪▶

SIZE
Instructions are written for size X-Small/Small.

MEASUREMENTS
BUST 33"/84cm
LENGTH 40½"/103cm
(excluding straps)

MATERIALS
• 9 1¾oz/50g hanks (each approx 170yd/156m) of Koigu *Premium Merino* (merino wool) in #2229 KPM light red (A)
• 7 hanks in #1100 KPM dark red (B)
• One pair size 2 (2.75mm) needles *or size to obtain gauge*
• Size C/2 (2.75mm) crochet hook

GAUGE
28 sts to 4"/10cm over garter st using size 2 (2.75mm) needles (before blocking).
➤ Take time to check gauge.

NOTES
1) Dress is made in one piece from the bottom up.
2) Straps are crocheted and added on last.
3) For skirt section, all A motifs are worked from the bottom up and all B motifs are worked from the top down, joining their edges to A motifs as you go.
4) For front and back sections, all motifs are worked from the bottom up.
5) Front section is longer than back section.

EYELET TRIANGLE
Row 1 (WS) K48, p1.
Row (dec) 2 (RS) Sl 1, k22, SK2P, k22, p1—47 sts.
Row 3 Sl 1, k22, p1, k22, p1.
Row 4 Sl 1, [k2tog, yo] 11 times, k1 (center st), [yo, k2tog] 11 times, p1.
Row 5 Sl 1, k22, p1, k22, p1.
Row (dec) 6 (RS) Sl 1, [k2tog, yo] 10 times, k1, SK2P, k1, [yo, k2tog] 10 times, p1—45 sts.
Row 7 Sl 1, k21, p1, k21, p1.
Row 8 Sl 1, [k2tog, yo] 10 times, k3, [yo, k2tog] 10 times, p1.
Row 9 Sl 1, k21, p1, k21, p1.
Row (dec) 10 (RS) Sl 1, [k2tog, yo] 10 times, SK2P, [yo, k2tog] 10 times, p1—43 sts.
Row 11 Sl 1, k20, p1, k20, p1.
Row 12 Sl 1, [k2tog, yo] 10 times, k1, [yo, k2tog] 10 times, p1.
Row 13 Sl 1, k20, p1, k20, p1.
Row (dec) 14 (RS) Sl 1, [k2tog, yo] 9 times, k1, SK2P, k1, [yo, k2tog] 9 times, p1—41 sts.
Row 15 Sl 1, k19, p1, k19, p1.
Row 16 Sl 1, [k2tog, yo] 9 times, k3, [yo, k2tog] 9 times, p1.
Row 17 Sl 1, k19, p1, k19, p1.
Row (dec) 18 (RS) Sl 1, [k2tog, yo] 9 times, SK2P, [yo, k2tog] 9 times, p1—39 sts.
Row 19 Sl 1, k18, p1, k18, p1.
Row 20 Sl 1, [k2tog, yo] 9 times, k1, [yo, k2tog] 9 times, p1.
Row 21 Sl 1, k18, p1, k18, p1.
Row (dec) 22 (RS) Sl 1, [k2tog, yo] 8 times, k1, SK2P, k1, [yo, k2tog] 8 times, p1—37 sts.
Row 23 Sl 1, k17, p1, k17, p1.
Row 24 Sl 1, [k2tog, yo] 8 times, k3, [yo, k2tog] 8 times, p1.
Row 25 Sl 1, k17, p1, k17, p1.
Row (dec) 26 (RS) Sl 1, [k2tog, yo] 8 times, SK2P, [yo, k2tog] 8 times, p1—35 sts.
Row 27 Sl 1, k16, p1, k16, p1.
Row 28 Sl 1, [k2tog, yo] 8 times, k1, [yo, k2tog] 8 times, p1.
Row 29 Sl 1, k16, p1, k16, p1.
Row (dec) 30 (RS) Sl 1, [k2tog, yo] 7 times, k1, SK2P, k1, [yo, k2tog] 7 times, p1—33 sts.
Row 31 Sl 1, k15, p1, k15, p1.
Row 32 Sl 1, [k2tog, yo] 7 times, k3, [yo, k2tog] 7 times, p1.
Row 33 Sl 1, k15, p1, k15, p1.
Row (dec) 34 (RS) Sl 1, [k2tog, yo] 7 times, SK2P, [yo, k2tog] 7 times, p1—31 sts.
Cont to dec 2 sts every 4th row as established until 11 sts rem, end with a WS row.
Next (dec) row (RS) Sl 1, k2tog, yo, k1, SK2P, k1, yo, k2tog, p1—9 sts.
Next row Sl 1, k3, p1, k3, p1.
Next (dec) row (RS) Sl 1, k2tog, yo, SK2P, yo, k2tog, p1—7 sts.
Next row Sl 1, k2, p1, k2, p1.
Next (dec) row (RS) Sl 1, k1, SK2P,

MAIE'S STORY
Maie Landra, mother of Taiu Landra (co-owner of Koigu Yarns), has been designing unique, colorful, and fashion-forward pieces for decades, and we don't expect her to stop anytime soon! Maie's late husband had his first heart attack when he was in his fifties, but by taking an active role in his heart health, he led a healthy life to the age of 80. For Maie, maintaining her excellent health is all about balance—eating foods that are natural to the source, avoiding processed foods, and staying hydrated by drinking plenty of liquids throughout the day. She enjoys an active life and likes to start every morning with exercise.

♥ MAIE'S TIP
YOU MAY BE ABLE TO SLEEP WHEN YOU'RE DEAD, but that might be sooner than you think if you cut those REM cycles short. Maie recommends getting eight hours of sleep every day so you can fully recover from a busy day of work, playing with the kids, or finishing your latest knitting project!

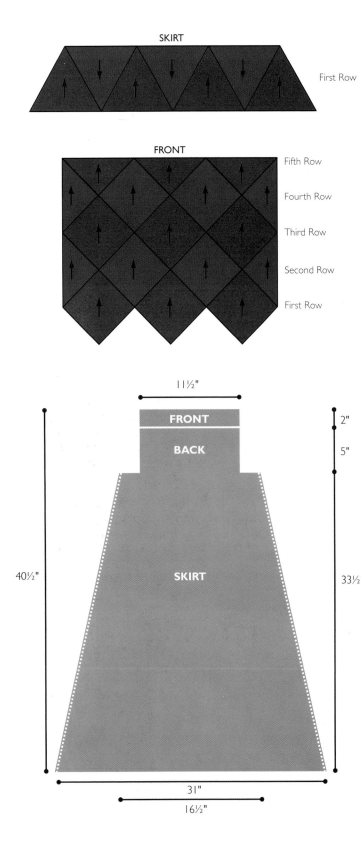

SKIRT

First Row

FRONT

Fifth Row
Fourth Row
Third Row
Second Row
First Row

BACK

Fourth Row
Third Row
Second Row
First Row

Measurements: 11½", 2", 5", 40½", 33½", 31", 16½" — FRONT, BACK, SKIRT

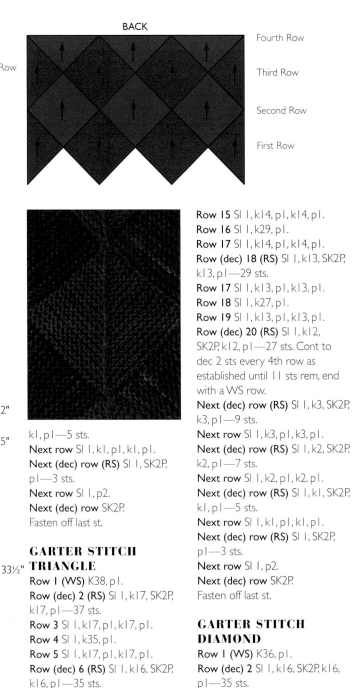

Row 15 Sl 1, k14, p1, k14, p1.
Row 16 Sl 1, k29, p1.
Row 17 Sl 1, k14, p1, k14, p1.
Row (dec) 18 (RS) Sl 1, k13, SK2P, k13, p1—29 sts.
Row 17 Sl 1, k13, p1, k13, p1.
Row 18 Sl 1, k27, p1.
Row 19 Sl 1, k13, p1, k13, p1.
Row (dec) 20 (RS) Sl 1, k12, SK2P, k12, p1—27 sts. Cont to dec 2 sts every 4th row as established until 11 sts rem, end with a WS row.
Next (dec) row (RS) Sl 1, k3, SK2P, k3, p1—9 sts.
Next row Sl 1, k3, p1, k3, p1.
Next (dec) row (RS) Sl 1, k2, SK2P, k2, p1—7 sts.
Next row Sl 1, k2, p1, k2, p1.
Next (dec) row (RS) Sl 1, k1, SK2P, k1, p1—5 sts.
Next row Sl 1, k1, p1, k1, p1.
Next (dec) row (RS) Sl 1, SK2P, p1—3 sts.
Next row Sl 1, p2.
Next (dec) row SK2P.
Fasten off last st.

GARTER STITCH DIAMOND

Row 1 (WS) K36, p1.
Row (dec) 2 Sl 1, k16, SK2P, k16, p1—35 sts.
Row 3 Sl 1, k16, p1, k16, p1.
Row (dec) 4 (RS) Sl 1, k15, SK2P, k15, p1—33 sts.
Row 5 Sl 1, k15, p1, k15, p1.
Row (dec) 6 (RS) Sl 1, k14, SK2P, k14, p1—31 sts.
Row 7 Sl 1, k14, p1, k14, p1.
Row (dec) 8 (RS) Sl 1, k13, SK2P, k13, p1—29 sts.
Row 9 Sl 1, k13, p1, k13, p1.

k1, p1—5 sts.
Next row Sl 1, k1, p1, k1, p1.
Next (dec) row (RS) Sl 1, SK2P, p1—3 sts.
Next row Sl 1, p2.
Next (dec) row SK2P.
Fasten off last st.

GARTER STITCH TRIANGLE

Row 1 (WS) K38, p1.
Row (dec) 2 (RS) Sl 1, k17, SK2P, k17, p1—37 sts.
Row 3 Sl 1, k17, p1, k17, p1.
Row 4 Sl 1, k35, p1.
Row 5 Sl 1, k17, p1, k17, p1.
Row (dec) 6 (RS) Sl 1, k16, SK2P, k16, p1—35 sts.
Row 7 Sl 1, k16, p1, k16, p1.
Row 8 Sl 1, k33, p1.
Row 9 Sl 1, k16, p1, k16, p1.
Row (dec) 10 (RS) Sl 1, k15, SK2P, k15, p1—33 sts.
Row 11 Sl 1, k15, p1, k15, p1.
Row 12 Sl 1, k31, p1.
Row 13 Sl 1, k15, p1, k15, p1.
Row (dec) 14 (RS) Sl 1, k14, SK2P, k14, p1—31 sts.

Row (dec) 10 (RS) Sl 1, k12, SK2P, k12, p1—27 sts. Cont to dec 2 sts every RS row as established until 11 sts rem, ending with a WS row.
Next (dec) row (RS) Sl 1, k3, SK2P, k3, p1—9 sts.
Next row Sl 1, k3, p1, k3, p1.
Next (dec) row (RS) Sl 1, k2, SK2P, k2, p1—7 sts.
Next row Sl 1, k2, p1, k2, p1.
Next (dec) row (RS) Sl 1, k1, SK2P, k1, p1—5 sts.
Next row Sl 1, k1, p1, k1, p1.
Next (dec) row (RS) Sl 1, SK2P, p1—3 sts.
Next row Sl 1, p2.
Next (dec) row SK2P.
Fasten off last st.

RIGHT-HALF GARTER STITCH DIAMOND
Row 1 (WS) Knit to last st, p1.
Row (dec) 2 (RS) K2tog, knit to last st, p1.
Rep rows 1 and 2 until 1 st rems.
Fasten off last st.

LEFT-HALF GARTER STITCH DIAMOND
Row 1 (WS) P1, knit to end.
Row (dec) row (RS) P1, knit to last 2 sts, k2tog.
Rep rows 1 and 2 until 1 st rems.
Fasten off last st.

SKIRT
The skirt is made of 5 rows of triangles. Each row is made of seven A triangles and seven B triangles. The first 4 rows are worked in eyelet triangle. The fifth row is worked in garter st triangle.

FIRST ROW
A EYELET TRIANGLES
(MAKE 7)
With A, cast on 49 sts using the backward loop method. Working first row through back lps, work eyelet triangle beg on row 1.

B EYELET TRIANGLES
With B, cast on 49 sts using the backward loop method. Working first row through back lps, work eyelet triangle as foll:
Row (joining) 1 (WS) K48, with WS of A triangle facing, purl last st on needle tog with last st at top of A triangle.
Row (dec/joining) 2 (RS) Sl 1, k22, SK2P, k22, with RS of a 2nd A triangle facing, purl last st on needle tog with last st at top of A triangle—47 sts (B triangle). Cont with row 3, cont to work eyelet triangle, joining edges to A triangles. Working in the same manner, cont to make and join B triangles to A triangles until all edges are joined.

SECOND ROW
A EYELET TRIANGLES
With RS of first row facing and A, pick up and k 22 sts evenly spaced from center st of a B triangle to center st of A triangle, pick up and k 1 st in center st, then pick up and k 22 sts to center st of next B triangle—45 sts. Beg with row 9, cont to work eyelet triangle. Working in the same manner, cont to make 6 more A triangles.

B EYELET TRIANGLES
With B, cast on 45 sts using the backward loop method. Working first row through back lps, work eyelet triangle as foll:
Row (joining) 9 (WS) Sl 1, k21, p1, k21, with WS of A triangle facing, purl last st on needle tog with last st at top of A triangle.
Row (dec/joining) 10 (RS) Sl 1, [k2tog, yo] 10 times, SK2P, [yo, k2tog] 10 times, with RS of a 2nd A triangle facing, purl last st on needle tog with last st at top of A triangle—43 sts (B triangle). Cont with row 11, cont to work B triangle, joining edges to A triangles. Working in the same manner, cont to make and join B triangles to A triangles until all edges are joined.

THIRD ROW
A EYELET TRIANGLES
With RS of second row facing and A, pick up and k 20 sts evenly spaced from center st of a B triangle to center st of A triangle, pick up and k 1 st in center st, then pick up and k 20 sts to center st of next B triangle—41 sts. Beg with row 17, cont to work eyelet triangle. Working in the same manner, cont to make 6 more A triangles.

B EYELET TRIANGLES
With B, cast on 41 sts using the backward loop method. Working first row through back lps, work eyelet triangle as foll:
Row (joining) 17 (WS) Sl 1, k19, p1, k19, with WS of A triangle facing, purl last st on needle tog with last st at top of a triangle.
Row (dec/joining) 18 (RS) Sl 1, [k2tog, yo] 9 times, SK2P, [yo, k2tog] 9 times, with RS of a 2nd A triangle facing, purl last st on needle tog with last st at top of A triangle—39 sts (B triangle). Cont with row 19, cont to work B triangle, joining edges to A triangles. Working in the same manner, cont to make and join B triangles to A triangles until all edges are joined.

FOURTH ROW
A EYELET TRIANGLES
With RS of third row facing and A, pick up and k 19 sts evenly spaced from center st of a B triangle to center st of A triangle, pick up and k 1 st in center st, then pick up and k 19 sts to center st of next B triangle—39 sts. Beg with row 19, cont to work eyelet triangle. Working in the same manner, cont to make 6 more A triangles.

B EYELET TRIANGLES
With B, cast on 39 sts using the backward loop method. Working first row through back lps, work eyelet triangle as foll:
Row (joining) 19 (WS) Sl 1, k18, p1, k18, with WS of A triangle facing, purl last st on needle tog with last st at top of A triangle.
Row (joining) 20 (RS) Sl 1, [k2tog, yo] 9 times, k1, [yo, k2tog] 9 times; with RS of a 2nd A triangle facing, purl last st on needle tog with last st at top of A triangle—39 sts (B triangle).
Cont with row 21, cont to work B triangle, joining edges to A triangles. Working in the same manner, cont to make and join B triangles to A triangles until all edges are joined.

FIFTH ROW
A GARTER ST TRIANGLES
With RS of fourth row facing and A, pick up and k 19 sts evenly spaced from center st of a B triangle to center st of A triangle, pick up and k 1 st in center st, then pick up and k 19 sts to center st of next B triangle—39 sts. Beg with row 1, cont to work garter st triangle. Working in the same manner, cont to make 6 more A triangles.

B GARTER ST TRIANGLES
With B, cast on 39 sts using the backward loop method. Working first row through back lps, work eyelet triangle as foll:
Row (joining) 1 (WS) Sl 1, k18, p1, k18, with WS of A triangle facing, purl last st on needle tog with last st at top of a triangle.
Row (dec/joining) 2 (RS) Sl 1, k17, SK2P, k17, with RS of a 2nd A triangle facing, purl last st on needle tog with last st at top of A triangle—37 sts (B triangle). Cont with row 3, cont to work B triangle, joining edges to A triangles. Working in the same manner, cont to make and join B triangles to A triangles until all edges are joined.

FRONT

The front is made of 5 rows of garter st diamonds. Each row is worked using one color. Follow diagram from right to left.

FIRST ROW

With RS of fifth row of skirt facing and A, pick up and k 18 sts evenly spaced from center st of a B triangle to center st of A triangle, pick up and k 1 st in center st, then pick up and k 18 sts to center st of next B triangle—37 sts. Beg with row 1, cont to work garter st diamond. Working from right to left, cont to make 2 more A diamonds.

SECOND ROW

With RS of first row of front facing and B, pick up and k 19 sts evenly spaced from RH corner of RH A garter st diamond to center st. Beg with row 1, cont to work right-half garter st diamond.
With RS of first row of front facing and B, pick up and k 37 sts evenly spaced from center st of RH A diamond to center st of center A diamond.
Beg with row 1, cont to work garter st diamond.
With RS of first row of front facing and B, pick up and k 37 sts evenly spaced from center st of center A diamond to center st of LH A diamond. Beg with row 1, cont to work garter st diamond.
With RS of first row of front facing and B, pick up and k 19 sts evenly spaced from center st of LH A diamond to LH corner. Beg with row 1, cont to work left-half garter st diamond.

THIRD ROW

With RS of second row of front facing and A, pick up and k 37 sts evenly spaced from center st of B right-half diamond to center st of next B diamond. Beg with row 1, cont to work garter st diamond. Working from right to left, cont to make 2 more A diamonds.

FOURTH ROW

With RS of third row of front facing and B, work same as second row.

FIFTH ROW

With RS of fourth row of front facing and A, pick up and k 37 sts evenly spaced from center st of B right-half diamond to center st of next B diamond. Beg with row 1, cont to work garter st diamond until 17 sts rem (half garter st diamond). Bind off knitwise. Working from right to left, cont to make 2 more A half garter st diamonds.

BACK

The back is made of 4 rows of garter st diamonds. Each row is worked using one color. Follow diagram from right to left.

FIRST ROW

Position skirt so RS is facing and front of dress is at back. To make first armhole opening, skip the top LH edge of the B garter st triangle of fifth row of skirt (the RH edge was used for the LH A garter st diamond motif on first row of front). With A, pick up and k 19 sts evenly spaced from RH corner to center st of next B garter st triangle. Beg with row 1, cont to work right-half garter st diamond.
With RS of fifth row of skirt facing and A, pick up and k 18 sts evenly spaced from center st of B triangle to center st of A triangle, pick up and k 1 st in center st, then pick up and k 18 sts to center st of next B triangle—37 sts. Beg with row 1, cont to work garter st diamond. Working from right to left, cont to make one more A diamond.
With RS of first row of front facing and A, pick up and k 19 sts evenly spaced from center st of LH B triangle to LH corner (RH edge skipped on the front makes the second armhole opening). Beg with row 1, cont to work left-half garter st diamond.

SECOND ROW

With RS of first row of back facing and B, pick up and k 37 sts evenly spaced from center st of A right-half diamond to center st of next A diamond. Beg with row 1, cont to work garter st diamond. Working from right to left, cont to make 2 more B diamonds.

THIRD ROW

With RS of second row of back facing and A, pick up and k 19 sts evenly spaced from RH corner of RH B garter st diamond to center st. Beg with row 1, cont to work right-half garter st diamond.
With RS of second row of back facing and A, pick up and k 37 sts evenly spaced from center st of RH B diamond to center st of center B diamond. Beg with row 1, cont to work garter st diamond. Working from right to left, make one more A garter st diamond.
With RS of second row of back facing and A, pick up and k 19 sts evenly spaced from center st of LH B diamond to LH corner. Beg with row 1, cont to work left-half garter st diamond.

FOURTH ROW

With RS of third row of front facing and B, pick up and k 37 sts evenly spaced from center st of A right-half diamond to center st of next A diamond. Beg with row 1, cont to work garter st diamond until 17 sts rem (half garter st diamond). Bind off knitwise. Working from right to left, cont to make 2 more B half garter st diamonds.

STRAPS (MAKE 2)

With crochet hook and A, ch 6.
Row 1 Sc in 2nd ch from hook and in each ch across—5 sc. Turn.
Row 2 Ch 1, sc in each st across. Turn. Rep row 2 until piiece measures 5½"/14cm from beg. Fasten off.

FINISHING

Wet block to measurements.

TOP EDGING

With RS facing and crochet hook, join A with a sl st in center of right underarm edge.
Rnd 1 (RS) Ch 1, making sure that work lies flat, sc evenly around entire edge, working 3 sc in each outer corner, join rnd with a sl st in first sc.
Rnd 2 (RS) Ch 1, sc in each st around, working 2 sc in center st of each outer corner, join rnd with a sl st in first sc. Fasten off.

BOTTOM EDGING

With RS facing and crochet hook, join A with a sl st in center back edge.
Rnd 1 (RS) Ch 1, making sure that work lies flat, sc evenly around entire edge, join rnd with a sl st in first sc. Fasten off. Sew on straps. ❤

Heart-healthy living

Information, tips, resources, and recipes

Get the facts!

In this book, you've read personal stories from knitting luminaries about their encounters with heart disease and how they look out for their own heart health. Here are some facts that everyone can use to learn more about heart disease and how to fight it.

RED ALERT!

Heart disease is the leading cause of death of women in the United States, but that sobering fact is not common knowledge. Here are a few more eye-opening statistics:

• Both men and women have heart attacks, but more women who have heart attacks die from them.

• Every 90 seconds, a woman in the United States has a heart attack.

• Among all U.S. women who die each year, one in four dies of heart disease.

• In 2004, nearly 60 percent more women died of cardiovascular disease (both heart disease and stroke) than from all cancers combined, and American women are 5 times more likely to die of heart disease than breast cancer.

• More than 10,000 American women younger than 45 have a heart attack every year.

Those are frightening figures, but the good news is that you can take steps to reduce your own risk of heart disease and educate loved ones to protect their hearts.

CHECK IT OUT

One good first step to heart healthiness is to find out how healthy your heart is right now. Here is a list of questions you should ask your doctor or nurse when you go for a physical:

What is my risk for heart disease and stroke?

Which screening or diagnostic tests for heart disease do I need, and when?

What can you do to help me quit smoking?

How much physical activity do I need to help protect my heart and blood vessels?

What is a heart-healthy eating plan for me?

What are my numbers and what do they mean?

☐ Blood pressure

☐ Cholesterol
• Total cholesterol
• LDL ("bad") cholesterol
• HDL ("good") cholesterol
• Triglycerides

☐ Body mass index and waist circumference measurement

☐ Blood sugar level

Once you have a baseline for your heart health, you will be able to track changes and improvements. Your doctor should also be able to tell you about various risk factors that may impact your heart health.

♥ DON'T SMOKE

IF YOU DON'T SMOKE, DON'T EVEN THINK ABOUT STARTING. Smoking carries many health risks beyond heart disease. If you do smoke, make every effort possible to quit. It's the best thing you can do for your health. Talk to your doctor about resources to help you quit, such as nicotine patches.

KNOW THE SIGNS

Knowing the signs of a heart attack and what to do when you experience them is one of the most important things you can do for your heart health.

For both women and men, the most common sympton of a heart attack is **pain or discomfort in the center of the chest.** The pain or discomfort can be mild or strong. It can last more than a few minutes, or it can go away and come back.

OTHER COMMON SIGNS OF A
HEART ATTACK INCLUDE:
- Pain or discomfort in one or both arms, back, neck, jaw, or stomach
- Shortness of breath (feeling like you can't get enough air). The shortness of breath often occurs before or along with the chest pain or discomfort.
- Nausea (feeling sick to your stomach) or vomiting
- Feeling faint or woozy
- Breaking out in a cold sweat
- Swelling in feet, ankles, and legs

Women are more likely than men to have these other common signs of a heart attack, particularly shortness of breath, nausea, or vomiting, and pain in the back, neck, or jaw.

WOMEN ARE ALSO MORE LIKELY TO HAVE LESS COMMON SIGNS OF A HEART ATTACK, INCLUDING:
**Heartburn • Loss of appetite • Fatigue or weakness
Coughing • Heart flutters**

The signs of a heart attack often occur suddenly, but they can also develop slowly over hours, days, and even weeks before a heart attack occurs. The more heart attack signs that you have, the more likely it is that you are having a heart attack.

Also, if you've already had a heart attack, your symptoms may not be the same for another one. Even if you're not sure you're having a heart attack, you should still have it checked out.

If you think you, or someone else, may be having a heart attack, wait no more than a few minutes—five at most—before calling 911.

EAT RIGHT FOR A HEALTHY HEART
Small changes in your diet can make a big difference in your heart health.

BEVERAGES
Take a break from sugary sodas and opt for water with lemon, unsweetened iced tea, or flavored water.

WHOLE GRAINS
Choose whole-grain breads, rice, and noodles, which are packed with important nutrients and are full of fiber to make you feel fuller faster.

SODIUM
Excess sodium has been linked to high blood pressure. Cut back on your sodium by limiting restaurant meals, avoiding processed foods, and using spices other than salt. There are plenty of salt-free spice combinations that you can find in your grocery store. It may take a while for you to get used to the taste, but eventually, you should lose your craving for salt.

POTASSIUM
A potassium-rich diet blunts the harmful effects of sodium on blood pressure. Foods rich in potassium include various fruits and vegetables, especially tomatoes and tomato products, orange juice and grapefruit juice, raisins, dates, and prunes, white potatoes and sweet potatoes, bananas, lettuce, and papayas.

APPETIZERS
Instead of being tempted by fried cheese sticks, opt for fresh fruit, sliced veggies, or salad. Salads should contain fresh greens, other fresh vegetables, and chickpeas. Pass on the high-fat and high-calorie nonvegetable choices, such as bacon, cheese, and croutons. And what better way to top it off than with lemon juice, vinegar, or a reduced-fat or fat-free dressing?

MAIN DISHES
When cooking at home or eating out, look for some key words on menus or in recipes to know you are making healthier choices. Terms like *skinless, broiled, baked, roasted, poached,* or *lightly sautéed* indicate foods that have been prepared in hearth-healthy ways.

FRUITS AND VEGETABLES
Try to eat at least five servings of fresh fruits and vegetables each day! Choose a variety of produce to maximize the nutritional benefits and keep your plate interesting.

DESSERTS
Although it's probably okay to order that French silk pie for a special occasion, there are plenty of other yummy alternatives to satisfy your sweet tooth. Try fresh fruit, fat-free frozen yogurt, sherbet, or sorbet. If you must indulge, split your dessert with a friend.

DON'T STRESS
Excess stress can raise your blood pressure and increase your risk of a heart attack. Find healthy ways to cope with stress. Lower your stress level by talking to your friends, exercising, or writing in a journal.

Exercise your heart

One of the best things you can do for your health is to get active!

Regular exercise can help to maintain a healthy body weight, lower blood pressure, and reduce stress—all of which will lower your risk for heart disease. The good news is that you don't have to run a marathon or climb a mountain. Each week aim to get at least:

❤ **2 HOURS AND 30 MINUTES OF MODERATE PHYSICAL ACTIVITY**
During moderate-intensity activities you should notice an increase in your heart rate, but you should still be able to talk comfortably. An example of a moderate-intensity activity is walking on a level surface at a brisk pace (about 3 to 4 miles per hour). Other examples include leisurely bicycling, and moderate housework.

OR

❤ **1 HOUR AND 15 MINUTES OF VIGOROUS PHYSICAL ACTIVITY**
If your heart rate increases a lot and you are breathing so hard that it is difficult to carry on a conversation, you are probably doing vigorous-intensity activity. Examples include jogging, bicycling fast or uphill, and singles tennis.

OR

❤ **A COMBINATION OF MODERATE AND VIGOROUS ACTIVITY**

AND

❤ **MUSCLE-STRENGTHENING ACTIVITIES ON TWO OR MORE DAYS**

ADDED BENEFITS

If you need more reasons to start moving, there is strong evidence that regular physical activity can also lower your risk of:

Stroke	Osteoporosis	Colon cancer
Type 2 diabetes	Depression	Breast cancer
High blood pressure	Unhealthy cholesterol levels	Lung cancer

MAKE TIME FOR YOU
Fun activities like yoga, cycling, and dancing the night away can reduce stress while exercising your heart!

READ ALL ABOUT IT!
Want to learn more? Here are some great resources for finding more information about heart disease and about the steps you can take to make your daily habits more heart healthy.

THE NATIONAL HEART, LUNG, AND
BLOOD INSTITUTE AND *THE HEART TRUTH*®
The Heart Truth is a national awareness and prevention campaign about heart disease in women sponsored by the National Heart, Lung, and Blood Institute (NHLBI), part of the National Institutes of Health of the U.S. Department of Health and Human Services. *The Heart Truth* campaign focuses on the following three areas: professional education, patient education, and public awareness.

CONTACT INFORMATION
www.nhlbi.nih.gov/educational/hearttruth
301-592-8573 • TTY: 240-629-3255
NHLBInfo@nhlbi.nih.gov

U.S. DEPARTMENT OF HEALTH AND HUMAN SERVICES
OFFICE ON WOMEN'S HEALTH
The Office on Women's Health (OWH) offers an award-winning comprehensive website that provide reliable, accurate, commercial-free information on the health of women. They cover more than 800 topics, on issues ranging from adolescent health to reproductive health to healthy aging.

CONTACT INFORMATION
200 Independence Avenue, S.W. , Washington, DC 20201
www.womenshealth.gov
800-994-9662 • TDD: 888-220-5446

ACT IN TIME TO HEART ATTACK SIGNS CAMPAIGN
The National Heart Attack Alert Program is an initiative of the National Heart, Lung, and Blood Institute to alert people to the signs of heart attack.

CONTACT INFORMATION
www.nhlbi.nih.gov/actintime
301-592-8573

♥ GO TO THE SOURCE
The above information was provided by the U.S. Department of Health and Human Services Office on Women's Health, which publishes helpful fact sheets:

HEART DISEASE FACT SHEET
www.womenshealth.gov/publications/our-publications/
fact-sheet/heart-disease.cfm

HEALTH SNAPSHOT: HEART DISEASE
www.womenshealth.gov/publications/our-publications/
fact-sheet/health-snapshot/heart-disease-health-snapshot.pdf

QUESTIONS TO ASK YOUR DOCTOR OR NURSE
www.womenshealth.gov/publications/our-publications/
heart-health-stroke-questions.pdf

HEART ATTACK FACTS: WHAT IS A HEART ATTACK?
www.womenshealth.gov/heartattack/facts.cfm?q=what
-is-a-heart-attack

PHYSICAL ACTIVITY (EXERCISE) FACT SHEET
www.womenshealth.gov/publications/our-publications/
fact-sheet/physical-activity.cfm

Heart-healthy eating doesn't have to be boring or flavorless. By making a few simple changes, you can lighten up your favorite recipes without sacrificing taste.

SOUPS

CORN CHOWDER

Here's a creamy chowder without the cream—or the fat.

INGREDIENTS

1 tablespoon vegetable oil

2 tablespoons celery, finely diced

2 tablespoons onion, finely diced

2 tablespoons green pepper, finely diced

1 package (10 ounces) frozen whole-kernel corn

1 cup raw potatoes, peeled, diced in ½-inch pieces

2 tablespoons fresh parsley, chopped

1 cup water

¼ teaspoon salt

Black pepper to taste

¼ teaspoon paprika

2 tablespoons flour

2 cups lowfat or skim milk

DIRECTIONS

1. Heat oil in medium saucepan. Add celery, onion, and green pepper, and sauté for 2 minutes.
2. Add corn, potatoes, water, salt, pepper, and paprika. Bring to boil, then reduce heat to medium. Cook covered for about 10 minutes or until potatoes are tender.
3. Place ½ cup of milk in jar with tight-fitting lid. Add flour and shake vigorously.
4. Gradually add milk-flour mixture to cooked vegetables. Then add remaining milk.
5. Cook, stirring constantly, until mixture comes to boil and thickens.
Serve garnished with chopped fresh parsley. ♥
➤ Yield: 4 servings • Serving size: 1 cup

NUTRITION INFORMATION

CALORIES:	186
TOTAL FAT:	5 GRAMS
SATURATED FAT:	1 GRAM
CHOLESTEROL:	5 MILLIGRAMS
SODIUM:	205 MILLIGRAMS
TOTAL FIBER:	4 GRAMS
PROTEIN:	7 GRAMS
CARBOHYDRATES:	31 GRAMS
POTASSIUM:	455 MILLIGRAMS

GAZPACHO

This classic soup is chock full of veggies.

INGREDIENTS

3 medium tomatoes, peeled, chopped

½ cup cucumber, seeded, chopped

½ cup green pepper, chopped

2 green onions, sliced

2 cups low-sodium vegetable juice cocktail

1 tablespoon lemon juice

½ teaspoon basil, dried

¼ teaspoon hot pepper sauce

1 clove garlic, minced

DIRECTIONS

1. In large mixing bowl, combine all ingredients.
2. Cover and chill for several hours. ♥
➤ Yield: 4 servings • Serving size: 1¼ cups

NUTRITION INFORMATION

CALORIES:	52
TOTAL FAT:	LESS THAN 1 GRAM
SATURATED FAT:	LESS THAN 1 GRAM
CHOLESTEROL:	0 MILLIGRAMS
SODIUM:	41 MILLIGRAMS
TOTAL FIBER:	2 GRAMS
PROTEIN:	2 GRAMS
CARBOHYDRATES:	12 GRAMS
POTASSIUM:	514 MILLIGRAMS

♥ SALAD DRESSINGS

VINAIGRETTE

Dress up your salad for a special meal with this delicious recipe.

INGREDIENTS

1 bulb garlic, separated into cloves, peeled

½ cup water

1 tablespoon red wine vinegar

¼ teaspoon honey

1 tablespoon virgin olive oil

½ teaspoon black pepper

DIRECTIONS

1. Place garlic cloves into small saucepan and pour in enough water (about ½ cup) to cover them.
2. Bring water to boil, then reduce heat and simmer until garlic is tender (about 15 minutes).
3. Reduce liquid to 2 tablespoons, and increase heat for 3 minutes.
4. Pour contents into small sieve over bowl. With wooden spoon, mash garlic through sieve.
5. Whisk vinegar into garlic mixture, then mix in oil and pepper. ♥
➤ Yield: 4 servings • Serving size: 2 tablespoons

NUTRITION INFORMATION

CALORIES:	33
TOTAL FAT:	3 GRAMS
SATURATED FAT:	1 GRAM
CHOLESTEROL:	0 MILLIGRAMS
SODIUM:	0 MILLIGRAMS
TOTAL FIBER:	0 GRAMS
PROTEIN:	0 GRAMS
CARBOHYDRATES:	1 GRAM
POTASSIUM:	9 MILLIGRAMS

FRESH SALSA

Fresh herbs add plenty of flavor to this salsa—so you use less salt.

INGREDIENTS

6 small (preferably Roma) or 3 large tomatoes
½ medium onion, finely chopped
1 clove garlic, finely minced
2 jalapeño peppers, finely chopped
3 tablespoons cilantro, chopped
Fresh lime juice to taste
⅛ teaspoon oregano, finely crushed
⅛ teaspoon salt
⅛ teaspoon pepper
½ avocado, diced

DIRECTIONS

1. Combine all ingredients in a glass bowl.
2. Serve immediately or refrigerate and serve within 4–5 hours. ❤

➤Yield: 8 servings • Serving size: ½ cup

NUTRITION INFORMATION

CALORIES: 42
TOTAL FAT: 2 GRAMS
SATURATED FAT: LESS THAN 1 GRAM
CHOLESTEROL: 0 MILLIGRAMS
SODIUM: 44 MILLIGRAMS
TOTAL FIBER: 2 GRAMS
PROTEIN: 1 GRAM
CARBOHYDRATES: 7 GRAMS
POTASSIUM: 337 MILLIGRAMS

MAIN DISHES

CRISPY OVEN-FRIED CHICKEN

Kids will love this chicken. It tastes batter-dipped and fried, but is actually good for the heart.

INGREDIENTS

½ cup skim milk or buttermilk
1 teaspoon poultry seasoning
1 cup cornflakes, crumbled
1½ tablespoons onion powder
1½ tablespoons garlic powder
2 teaspoons black pepper
2 teaspoons dried hot pepper, crushed
1 teaspoon ginger, ground
8 pieces chicken, skinless
  (4 breasts, 4 drumsticks)
A few shakes of paprika
1 teaspoon vegetable oil

DIRECTIONS

1. Preheat oven to 350°F.
2. Add ½ teaspoon of poultry seasoning to milk.
3. Combine all other spices with cornflake crumbs and place in plastic bag.
4. Wash chicken and pat dry. Dip chicken into milk, shake to remove excess, then quickly shake in bag with seasoning and crumbs.
5. Refrigerate for 1 hour.
6. Remove from refrigerator and sprinkle lightly with paprika for color.
7. Evenly space chicken on greased baking pan.
8. Cover with aluminum foil and bake for 40 minutes. Remove foil and continue baking for an added 30–40 minutes, or until meat can be easily pulled away from bone with fork. Drumsticks may require less baking time than breasts. (Do not turn chicken during baking.) Crumbs will form a crispy "skin." ❤

➤Yield: 6 servings • Serving size: ½ breast or 2 small drumsticks

NUTRITION INFORMATION

CALORIES: 256
TOTAL FAT: 5 GRAMS
SATURATED FAT: 1 GRAM
CHOLESTEROL: 82 MILLIGRAMS
SODIUM: 286 MILLIGRAMS
TOTAL FIBER: 1 GRAM
PROTEIN: 30 GRAMS
CARBOHYDRATES: 22 GRAMS
POTASSIUM: 339 MILLIGRAMS

TURKEY MEAT LOAF

Here's a healthier version of an old diner favorite.

INGREDIENTS

1 pound lean turkey, ground
½ cup regular oats, dry
1 large egg
1 tablespoon onion, dehydrated
¼ cup ketchup

DIRECTIONS

1. Combine all ingredients and mix well.
2. Bake in loaf pan at 350°F, or to internal temperature of 165°F, for 25 minutes.
3. Cut into five slices and serve. ❤

➤Yield: 5 servings • Serving size: 1 slice (3 ounces)

NUTRITION INFORMATION

CALORIES: 192
TOTAL FAT: 7 GRAMS
SATURATED FAT: 2 GRAMS
CHOLESTEROL: 103 MILLIGRAMS
SODIUM: 214 MILLIGRAMS
TOTAL FIBER: 1 GRAM
PROTEIN: 21 GRAMS
CARBOHYDRATES: 23 GRAMS
POTASSIUM: 292 MILLIGRAMS

❤KEEP COOKING!
These fabulous recipes were provided by the National Heart, Lung, and Blood Institute. For more delicious, heart-healthy recipes, go to: www.nhlbi.nih.gov/health/public/heart/other/ktb_recipebk/ktb_recipebk.pdf

BEEF STROGANOFF

Lean top-round beef and plain low-fat yogurt transform this rich dish into a heart-healthy meal. Swapping macaroni for the traditional egg noodles reduces the fat.

INGREDIENTS

1 pound lean beef (top round), cubed

2 teaspoons vegetable oil

¾ tablespoon onion, finely chopped

1 pound mushrooms, sliced

¼ teaspoon salt

Pepper to taste

¼ teaspoon nutmeg

½ teaspoon dried basil

¼ cup white wine

1 cup plain lowfat yogurt

6 cups macaroni, cooked in unsalted water

DIRECTIONS

1. Cut beef into 1-inch cubes.
2. Heat 1 teaspoon oil in nonstick skillet. Add onion and sauté for 2 minutes.
3. Add beef and sauté for 5 minutes more. Turn to brown evenly. Remove from pan and keep hot.
4. Add remaining oil to pan and sauté mushrooms.
5. Add beef and onions to pan with seasonings.
6. Add wine and yogurt, and gently stir in. Heat, but do not boil.*
7. Serve with macaroni.

* If thickening is desired, use 2 teaspoons of cornstarch. Calories are same as for flour, but cornstarch has double the thickening power. The calories for cornstarch are not included in the nutrients per serving given above. To add cornstarch, take a small amount of wine-and-yogurt broth and put aside to cool. Stir in cornstarch. Add some of warm broth to cornstarch paste and stir. Then, add cornstarch mixture to pan. ♥

➤Yield: 5 servings • Serving size: 6 ounces

NUTRITION INFORMATION

CALORIES: 499

TOTAL FAT: 10 GRAMS

SATURATED FAT: 3 GRAMS

CHOLESTEROL: 80 MILLIGRAMS

SODIUM: 200 MILLIGRAMS

TOTAL FIBER: 4 GRAMS

PROTEIN: 41 GRAMS

CARBOHYDRATES: 58 GRAMS

POTASSIUM: 891 MILLIGRAMS

CHICKEN SALAD

Chill out with this simple, yet flavorful dish.

INGREDIENTS

3¼ cups chicken, cooked, cubed, skinless

¼ cup celery, chopped

1 tablespoon lemon juice

½ teaspoon onion powder

1/8 teaspoon salt*

3 tablespoons lowfat mayonnaise

DIRECTIONS

1. Bake chicken, cut into cubes, and refrigerate.
2. In large bowl, combine rest of ingredients, add chilled chicken, and mix well. ♥
*Reduce sodium by removing the ⅛ teaspoon of added salt. New sodium content for each serving is 127 milligrams.

➤Yield: 5 servings • Serving size: ¾ cup

NUTRITION INFORMATION

CALORIES: 183

TOTAL FAT: 7 GRAMS

SATURATED FAT: 2 GRAMS

CHOLESTEROL: 78 MILLIGRAMS

SODIUM: 201 MILLIGRAMS

TOTAL FIBER: 0 GRAMS

PROTEIN: 27 GRAMS

CARBOHYDRATES: 1 GRAM

POTASSIUM: 240 MILLIGRAMS

CHICKEN AND RICE

Let this Latin-inspired dish—full of heart-healthy ingredients—inspire you.

INGREDIENTS

6 chicken pieces (legs and breasts), skin removed

2 teaspoons vegetable oil

4 cups water

2 tomatoes, chopped

½ cup green pepper, chopped

¼ cup red pepper, chopped

¼ cup celery, diced

1 medium carrot, grated

¼ cup corn, frozen

½ cup onion, chopped

¼ cup fresh cilantro, chopped

2 cloves garlic, chopped fine

⅛ teaspoon salt

⅛ teaspoon pepper

2 cups rice

¼ cup frozen peas

2 ounces Spanish olives

¼ cup raisins

DIRECTIONS

1. In large pot, brown chicken pieces in oil.
2. Add water, tomatoes, green and red peppers, celery, carrots, corn, onion, cilantro, garlic, salt, and pepper. Cover and cook over medium heat for 20–30 minutes or until chicken is done.
3. Remove chicken from pot and place in refrigerator. Add rice, peas, and olives to pot. Cover pot and cook over low heat for about 20 minutes, until rice is done.
4. Add chicken and raisins, and cook for another 8 minutes. Enjoy! ♥

➤Yield: 6 servings • Serving size: 1 cup of rice and 1 piece of chicken

NUTRITION INFORMATION

CALORIES: 448

TOTAL FAT: 7 GRAMS

SATURATED FAT: 2 GRAMS

CHOLESTEROL: 49 MILLIGRAMS

SODIUM: 352 MILLIGRAMS

TOTAL FIBER: 4 GRAMS

PROTEIN: 24 GRAMS

CARBOHYDRATES: 70 GRAMS

POTASSIUM: 551 MILLIGRAMS

SHISH KABOBS

The delicious taste of these kabobs comes from the lively marinade, which features wine, lemon juice, rosemary, and garlic.

INGREDIENTS

2 tablespoons olive oil

½ cup chicken broth

¼ cup red wine

1 lemon, juice only

1 teaspoon chopped garlic

¼ teaspoon salt

½ teaspoon rosemary

⅛ teaspoon black pepper

2 pounds lean lamb, cut into 1-inch cubes

24 cherry tomatoes

24 mushrooms

24 small onions

DIRECTIONS

1. Combine oil, broth, wine, lemon juice, garlic, salt, rosemary, and pepper. Pour over lamb, tomatoes, mushrooms, and onions. Marinate in refrigerator for several hours or overnight.
2. Put together skewers of lamb, onions, mushrooms, and tomatoes. Broil 3 inches from heat for 15 minutes, turning every 5 minutes. ❤

➤ Yield: 8 servings • Serving size: 1 kabob, with 3 ounces of meat

NUTRITION INFORMATION

CALORIES: 274

TOTAL FAT: 12 GRAMS

SATURATED FAT: 3 GRAMS

CHOLESTEROL: 75 MILLIGRAMS

SODIUM: 207 MILLIGRAMS

TOTAL FIBER: 3 GRAMS

PROTEIN: 26 GRAMS

CARBOHYDRATES: 16 GRAMS

POTASSIUM: 728 MILLIGRAMS

OVEN-FRIED FISH

This heart-healthy entrée can be made with many kinds of fish.

INGREDIENTS

2 pounds fish fillets

1 tablespoon lemon juice, fresh

¼ cup skim milk or 1% buttermilk

2 drops hot pepper sauce

1 teaspoon fresh garlic, minced

¼ teaspoon white pepper, ground

¼ teaspoon salt

¼ teaspoon onion powder

¼ cup cornflakes, crumbled, or bread crumbs

1 tablespoon vegetable oil

1 fresh lemon, cut into wedges

DIRECTIONS

1. Preheat oven to 475°F.
2. Wipe fillets with lemon juice and pat dry.
3. Combine milk, hot pepper sauce, and garlic.
4. Combine pepper, salt, and onion powder with cornflake crumbs and place on plate.
5. Let fillets sit briefly in milk. Remove and coat fillets on both sides with seasoned crumbs. Let stand briefly until coating sticks to each side of fish.
6. Arrange on lightly oiled shallow baking dish.
7. Bake for 20 minutes on middle rack without turning.
8. Cut into 6 pieces. Serve with fresh lemon. ❤

➤ Yield: 6 servings • Serving size: 1 cut piece

NUTRITION INFORMATION

CALORIES: 183

TOTAL FAT: 2 GRAMS

SATURATED FAT: LESS THAN 1 GRAM

CHOLESTEROL: 80 MILLIGRAMS

SODIUM: 325 MILLIGRAMS

TOTAL FIBER: 1 GRAM

PROTEIN: 30 GRAMS

CARBOHYDRATES: 10 GRAMS

POTASSIUM: 453 MILLIGRAMS

SIDE DISHES

ITALIAN VEGETABLE BAKE

Try this colorful, low-sodium baked dish, prepared without added fat.

INGREDIENTS

1 can (28 ounces) tomatoes, whole

1 medium onion, sliced

½ pound fresh green beans, sliced

½ pound fresh okra, cut into ½-inch pieces
   (or ½ of 10-ounce package frozen, cut)

¾ cup green pepper, finely chopped

2 tablespoons lemon juice

1 tablespoon fresh basil, chopped
   (or 1 teaspoon dried basil, crushed)

1½ teaspoons fresh oregano leaves, chopped
   (or ½ teaspoon dried oregano, crushed)

3 medium (7-inch-long) zucchini,
   cut into 1-inch cubes

1 medium eggplant, pared,
   cut into 1-inch cubes

2 tablespoons Parmesan cheese, grated

DIRECTIONS

1. Drain and coarsely chop tomatoes. Save liquid. Mix together tomatoes, reserved liquid, onion, green beans, okra, green pepper, lemon juice, and herbs. Cover and bake at 325°F for 15 minutes.
2. Mix in zucchini and eggplant. Continue baking, covered, stirring occasionally, 60–70 minutes more, or until vegetables are tender.
3. Just before serving, sprinkle top with Parmesan cheese. ❤

➤ Yield: 18 servings • Serving size: ½ cup

NUTRITION INFORMATION

CALORIES: 27

TOTAL FAT: LESS THAN 1 GRAM

SATURATED FAT: LESS THAN 1 GRAM

CHOLESTEROL: 1 MILLIGRAM

SODIUM: 86 MILLIGRAMS

TOTAL FIBER: 2 GRAMS

PROTEIN: 2 GRAMS

CARBOHYDRATES: 5 GRAMS

POTASSIUM: 244 MILLIGRAMS

▲ Greenmarket Tote (page 72)

OVEN FRENCH FRIES

Find French fries hard to resist? Here's a version to give in to!

INGREDIENTS

4 large potatoes (2 pounds)
8 cups ice water
1 teaspoon garlic powder
1 teaspoon onion powder
¼ teaspoon salt
1 teaspoon white pepper
¼ teaspoon allspice
1 teaspoon hot pepper flakes
1 tablespoon vegetable oil

DIRECTIONS

1. Scrub potatoes and cut into ½-inch strips.
2. Place potato strips into ice water, cover, and chill for 1 hour or longer.
3. Remove potatoes and dry strips thoroughly.
4. Place garlic powder, onion powder, salt, white pepper, allspice, and pepper flakes in plastic bag.
5. Toss potatoes in spice mixture.
6. Brush potatoes with oil.
7. Place potatoes in nonstick shallow baking pan.
8. Cover with aluminum foil and place in 475°F oven for 15 minutes.
9. Remove foil and continue baking uncovered for additional 15–20 minutes or until golden brown. Turn fries occasionally to brown on all sides. ❤

➤ Yield: 5 servings • Serving size: 1 cup

NUTRITION INFORMATION

CALORIES: 238
TOTAL FAT: 4 GRAMS
SATURATED FAT: 1 GRAM
CHOLESTEROL: 0 MILLIGRAMS
SODIUM: 163 MILLIGRAMS
TOTAL FIBER: 5 GRAMS
PROTEIN: 5 GRAMS
CARBOHYDRATES: 48 GRAMS
POTASSIUM: 796 MILLIGRAMS

DESSERTS

PEACH COBBLER

What could be better than peach cobbler straight from the oven? A healthier version of the classic favorite!

INGREDIENTS

½ teaspoon ground cinnamon

1 tablespoon vanilla extract

2 tablespoons cornstarch

1 cup peach nectar

¼ cup pineapple juice or peach juice (if desired, use juice reserved from canned peaches)

2 cans (16 ounces each) peaches, packed in juice, drained, sliced (or 1¾ pounds fresh)

1 tablespoon tub margarine

1 cup dry pancake mix

⅔ cup all-purpose flour

½ cup sugar

⅔ cup evaporated skim milk

Nonstick cooking spray as needed

½ teaspoon nutmeg

1 tablespoon brown sugar

DIRECTIONS

1. Combine cinnamon, vanilla, cornstarch, peach nectar, and pineapple or peach juice in saucepan over medium heat. Stir constantly until mixture thickens and bubbles.
2. Add sliced peaches to mixture.
3. Reduce heat and simmer for 5–10 minutes.
4. In another saucepan, melt margarine and set aside.
5. Lightly spray 8-inch-square glass dish with cooking spray. Pour hot peach mixture into dish.
6. In another bowl, combine pancake mix, flour, sugar, and melted margarine. Stir in milk. Quickly spoon this over peach mixture.
7. Combine nutmeg and brown sugar. Sprinkle on top of batter.
8. Bake at 400°F for 15–20 minutes or until golden brown.
9. Cool and cut into 8 pieces. ❤

➤ Yield: 8 servings • Serving size: 1 piece

NUTRITION INFORMATION

CALORIES: 271

TOTAL FAT: 4 GRAMS

SATURATED FAT: LESS THAN 1 GRAM

CHOLESTEROL: LESS THAN 1 MILLIGRAM

SODIUM: 263 MILLIGRAMS

TOTAL FIBER: 2 GRAMS

PROTEIN: 4 GRAMS

CARBOHYDRATES: 54 GRAMS

POTASSIUM: 284 MILLIGRAMS

BANANA MOUSSE

This creamy dessert only tastes like it's high in fat.

INGREDIENTS

2 tablespoons lowfat milk

4 teaspoons sugar

1 teaspoon vanilla

1 medium banana, cut into quarters

1 cup plain lowfat yogurt

8 slices (¼ inch each) banana

DIRECTIONS

1. Place milk, sugar, vanilla, and banana in blender. Process for 15 seconds at high speed until smooth.
2. Pour mixture into small bowl and fold in yogurt. Chill.
3. Spoon into four dessert dishes and garnish each with two banana slices just before serving. ❤

➤ Yield: 4 servings • Serving size: ½ cup

NUTRITION INFORMATION

CALORIES: 94

TOTAL FAT: 1 GRAM

SATURATED FAT: 1 GRAM

CHOLESTEROL: 4 MILLIGRAMS

SODIUM: 47 MILLIGRAMS

TOTAL FIBER: 1 GRAM

PROTEIN: 1 GRAM

CARBOHYDRATES: 18 GRAMS

POTASSIUM: 297 MILLIGRAMS

RICE PUDDING

Skim milk gives a whole lot of flavor without whole milk's fat and calories.

INGREDIENTS

6 cups water

2 sticks cinnamon

1 cup rice

3 cups skim milk

⅔ cup sugar

½ teaspoon salt

DIRECTIONS

1. Put water and cinnamon sticks into medium saucepan. Bring to boil.
2. Stir in rice. Cook on low heat for 30 minutes, until rice is soft and water has evaporated.
3. Add skim milk, sugar, and salt. Cook for another 15 minutes until mixture thickens. ❤

➤ Yield: 5 servings • Serving size: ½ cup

NUTRITION INFORMATION

CALORIES: 372

TOTAL FAT: 1 GRAM

SATURATED FAT: LESS THAN 1 GRAM

CHOLESTEROL: 3 MILLIGRAMS

SODIUM: 366 MILLIGRAMS

TOTAL FIBER: 1 GRAM

PROTEIN: 10 GRAMS

CARBOHYDRATES: 81 GRAMS

POTASSIUM: 363 MILLIGRAMS

knitting know-how

ABBREVIATIONS

approx	approximately	rem	remain(s)(ing)
beg	begin(ning)	rep	repeat
CC	contrasting color	RH	right-hand
ch	chain	RS	right side(s)
cm	centimeter(s)	rnd(s)	round(s)
cn	cable needle	SKP	slip 1, knit 1, pass slip stitch over—
cont	continu(e)(ing)		one stitch has been decreased
dec	decreas(e)(ing)	SK2P	slip 1, knit 2 together, pass slip
dpn	double-pointed needle(s)		stitch over the knit 2 together—
foll	follow(s)(ing)		two stitches have been
g	gram(s)		decreased
inc	increas(e)(ing)	S2KP	slip 2 stitches together, knit 1, pass
k	knit		2 slip stitches over knit 1
kfb	knit into the front and back of a	sl	slip
	stitch—one stitch has been	sl st	slip stitch (see glossary)
	increased	ssk	slip, slip, knit (see glossary)
k2tog	knit 2 stitches together—one stitch	sssk	slip, slip, slip, knit (see glossary)
	has been decreased	st(s)	stitch(es)
LH	left-hand	St st	stockinette stitch
lp(s)	loop(s)	tbl	through back loop(s)
m	meter(s)	tog	together
mm	millimeter(s)	WS	wrong side(s)
MC	main color	wyib	with yarn in back
M1	make one (see glossary)	wyif	with yarn in front
M1 p-st	make 1 purl stitch (see glossary)	yd	yard(s)
oz	ounce(s)	yo	yarn over needle (U.K.: see
p	purl		glossary)
pat(s)	pattern(s)	*	repeat directions following * as
pm	place marker (see glossary)		many times as indicated
psso	pass slip stitch(es) over	[ ]	repeat directions inside brackets as
p2tog	purl two stitches together—one		many times as indicated
	stitch has been decreased		

KNITTING NEEDLES

US	METRIC
0	2mm
1	2.25mm
2	2.75mm
3	3.25mm
4	3.5mm
5	3.75mm
6	4mm
7	4.5mm
8	5mm
9	5.5mm
10	6mm
10 ½	6.5mm
11	8mm
13	9mm
15	10mm
17	12.75mm
19	15mm
35	19mm

SKILL LEVELS

 1. BEGINNER
Ideal first project.

2. EASY
Basic stitches, minimal shaping, and simple finishing.

3. INTERMEDIATE
For knitters with some experience. More intricate stitches, shaping, and finishing.

4. EXPERIENCED
For knitters able to work patterns with complicated shaping and finishing.

GAUGE

Make a test swatch at least 4"/10cm square. If the number of stitches and rows does not correspond to the gauge given, you must change the needle size.

AN EASY RULE TO FOLLOW IS: To get fewer stitches to the inch/cm, use a larger needle; to get more stitches to the inch/cm, use a smaller needle. Continue to try different needle sizes until you get the same number of stitches in the gauge.

Stitches measured over 4"/5cm.

Rows measured over 4"/5cm.

GLOSSARY

bind off Used to finish an edge or segment. Lift the first stitch over the second, the second over the third, etc. (U.K.: cast off)

bind off in ribbing Work in ribbing as you bind off. (Knit the knit stitches, purl the purl stitches.) (U.K.: cast off in ribbing)

cast on Placing a foundation row of stitches upon the needle in order to begin knitting.

decrease Reduce the stitches in a row (that is, knit 2 together).

increase Add stitches in a row (that is, knit in front and back of stitch).

knitwise Insert the needle into the stitch as if you were going to knit it.

make one With the needle tip, lift the strand between the last stitch knit and the next stitch on the left-hand needle and knit into back of it. One knit stitch has been added.

make one p-st With the needle tip, lift the strand between the last stitch worked and the next stitch on the left-hand needle and purl it. One purl stitch has been added.

no stitch On some charts, "no stitch" is indicated with shaded spaces where stitches have been decreased or not yet made. In such cases, work the stitches of the chart, skipping over the "no stitch" spaces.

place markers Place or attach a loop of contrast yarn or purchased stitch marker as indicated.

pick up and knit (purl) Knit (or purl) into the loops along an edge.

purlwise Insert the needle into the stitch as if you were going to purl it.

selvage stitch Edge stitch that helps make seaming easier.

slip, slip, knit Slip next two stitches knitwise, one at a time, to right-hand needle. Insert tip of left-hand needle into fronts of these stitches, from left to right. Knit them together. One stitch has been decreased.

slip, slip, slip, knit Slip next three stitches knitwise, one at a time, to right-hand needle. Insert tip of left-hand needle into fronts of these stitches, from left to right. Knit them together. Two stitches have been decreased.

slip stitch An unworked stitch made by passing a stitch from the left-hand to the right-hand needle as if to purl.

work even Continue in pattern without increasing or decreasing. (U.K.: work straight)

yarn over Making a new stitch by wrapping the yarn over the right-hand needle. (U.K.: yfwd, yon, yrn)

Standard yarn weight system

Categories of yarn, gauge ranges, and recommended needle and hook sizes

Yarn Weight Symbol & Category Names	0 Lace	1 Super Fine	2 Fine	3 Light	4 Medium	5 Bulky	6 Super Bulky
Type of Yarns in Category	Fingering 10 count crochet thread	Sock, Fingering, Baby	Sport, Baby	DK, Light Worsted	Worsted, Afghan, Aran	Chunky, Craft, Rug	Bulky, Roving
Knit Gauge Range* in Stockinette Stitch to 4 inches	33–40** sts	27–32 sts	23–26 sts	21–24 sts	16–20 sts	12–15 sts	6–11 sts
Recommended Needle in Metric Size Range	1.5–2.25 mm	2.25–3.25 mm	3.25–3.75 mm	3.75–4.5 mm	4.5–5.5 mm	5.5–8 mm	8 mm and larger
Recommended Needle U.S. Size Range	000 to 1	1 to 3	3 to 5	5 to 7	7 to 9	9 to 11	11 and larger
Crochet Gauge* Ranges in Single Crochet to 4 inch	32-42 double crochets**	21–32 sts	16–20 sts	12–17 sts	11–14 sts	8–11 sts	5–9 sts
Recommended Hook in Metric Size Range	Steel*** 1.6–1.4mm Regular hook 2.25 mm	2.25–3.5 mm	3.5–4.5 mm	4.5–5.5 mm	5.5–6.5 mm	6.5–9 mm	9 mm and larger
Recommended Hook U.S. Size Range	Steel*** 6, 7, 8 Regular hook B–1	B–1 to E–4	E–4 to 7	7 to I–9	I–9 to K–10½	K–10½ to M–13	M–13 and larger

* Guidelines only: The above reflect the most commonly used gauges and needle or hook sizes for specific yarn categories.

** Lace weight yarns are usually knitted or crocheted on larger needles and hooks to create lacy, openwork patterns. Accordingly, a gauge range is difficult to determine. Always follow the gauge stated in your pattern.

*** Steel crochet hooks are sized differently from regular hooks—the higher the number, the smaller the hook, which is the reverse of regular hook sizing.

METRIC CONVERSIONS To convert measurements from inches to centimeters, simply multiply by 2.54.

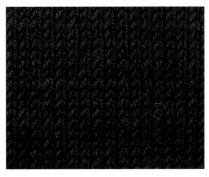

BASIC STITCHES
Garter stitch
Knit every row. Circular knitting: Knit one round, then purl one round.

Stockinette stitch
Knit right-side rows and purl wrong-side rows. Circular knitting: Knit all rounds.
(U.K.: stocking stitch)

Seed stitch
Row 1 *K1, p1, repeat from * to end.
Row 2 *P1, k1; repeat from * to end.
Repeat rows 1 and 2.
(U.K.: moss stitch)

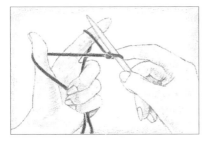

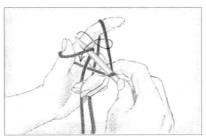

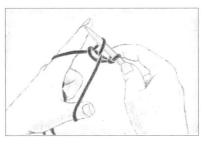

LONG-TAIL CAST-ON
1. Make a slip knot on the right needle, leaving a long tail. Wind the tail end around your left thumb, front to back. Wrap the yarn from the ball over your left index finger and secure the ends in your palm.

2. Insert the needle upward in the loop on your thumb. Then with the needle, draw the yarn from the ball through the loop to form a stitch.

3. Take your thumb out of the loop and tighten the loop on the needle. Continue in this way until all the stitches are cast on.

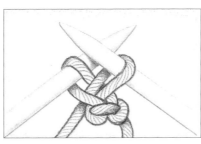

KNITTING ON CAST-ON
1. Make a slip knot on the left needle. *Insert the right needle knitwise into the stitch on the left needle. Wrap the yarn around the right needle as if to knit.

2. Draw the yarn through the first stitch to make a new stitch, but do not drop the stitch from the left needle.

3. Slip the new stitch to the left needle as shown. Repeat from the * until the required number of stitches is cast on.

CABLE CAST-ON
Cast on two stitches using the knitting-on cast-on described on page 120. *Insert the right needle between the two stitches on the left needle.

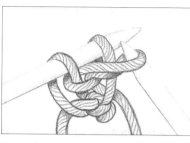

Wrap the yarn around the right needle as if to knit and pull the yarn through to make a new stitch.

Place the new stitch on the left needle as shown. Repeat from the *, always inserting the right needle in between the last two stitches on the left needle.

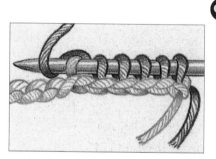

CHAIN-STITCH PROVISIONAL CAST-ON
With waste yarn, make a crochet chain a few stitches longer than the number of stitches to be cast on. With main-color yarn, pick up one stitch in the back loop of each chain. To knit from the cast-on edge, carefully unpick the chain, placing the live stitches one by one on a needle.

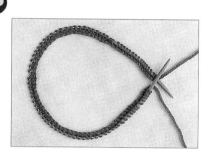

KNITTING WITH CIRCULAR NEEDLES
Cast on as you would for straight knitting. Distribute the stitches evenly around the needle, being sure not to twist them. The last cast-on stitch is the last stitch of the round. Place a marker here to indicate the end of the round.

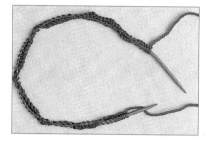

If the cast-on stitches are twisted, as shown, you will find that after you knit a few inches the fabric will be twisted.

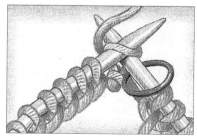

1. Hold the needle tip with the last cast-on stitch in your right hand and the tip with the first cast-on stitch in your left hand. Knit the first cast-on stitch, pulling the yarn tight to avoid a gap.

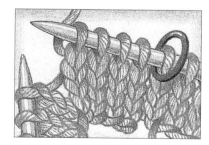

2. Work until you reach the marker. This completes the first round. Slip the marker to the right needle and work the next round.

KNITTING WITH DPNS
Cast-on with three needles.

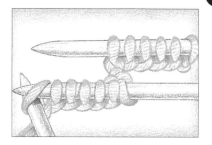

1. Cast on the required number of stitches on the first needle, plus one extra. Slip this extra stitch to the next needle as shown. Continue in this way, casting on the required number of stitches on the last needle.

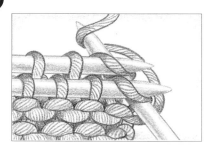

3-NEEDLE BIND-OFF
1. With the right side of the two pieces facing each other, and the needles parallel, insert a third needle knitwise into the first stitch of each needle. Wrap the yarn around the needle as if to knit.

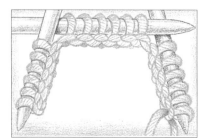

2. Arrange the needles as shown, with the cast-on edge facing the center of the triangle (or square).

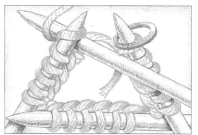

3. Place a stitch marker after the last cast-on stitch. With the fee needle, knit the first cast-on stitch, pulling the yarn tightly. Continue knitting in rounds, slipping the marker before beginning each round.

2. Knit these two stitches together and slip them off the needles. *Knit the next two stitches together in the same way as shown.

▲ Multipattern Mittens (page 68)

3. Slip the first stitch on the third needle over the second stitch and off the needle. Repeat from the * in step 2 across the row until all the stitches are bound off.

▲ Cabled Cardi (page 39)

▲ Cabled Knee-Highs (page 57)

▲ Leaf Lace Sweater (page 46)

CABLES

Front (or Left) Cable

1. Slip the first three stitches of the cable purlwise to a cable needle and hold them to the front of the work. Be careful not to twist the stitches.

2. Leave the stitches suspended in front of the work, keeping them in the center of the cable needle where they won't slip off. Pull the yarn firmly and knit the next three stitches.

3. Knit the three stitches from the cable needle. If this seems too awkward, return the stitches to the left needle and then knit them.

Back (or Right) Cable

1. Slip the first three stitches of the cable purlwise to a cable needle and hold them to the back of the work. Be careful not to twist the stitches.

2. Leave the stitches suspended in back of the work, keeping them in the center of the cable needle where they won't slip off. Pull the yarn firmly and knit the next three stitches.

3. Knit the three stitches from the cable needle. If this seems too awkward, return the stitches to the left needle and then knit them.

YARN OVERS

There are different ways to make a yarn over. Which method to use depends on where you are in the stitch pattern. If you do not make the yarn over in the right way, you may lose it on the following row, or make a yarn over that is too big. Here are the different variations:

Between two knit stitches:
Bring the yarn from the back of the work to the front between the two needles. Knit the next stitch, bringing the yarn to the back over the right-hand needle, as shown.

Between a knit and a purl stitch:
Bring the yarn from the back to the front between the two needles. Then bring it to the back over the right-hand needle and back to the front again, as shown. Purl the next stitch.

Between a purl and a knit stitch: Leave the yarn at the front of the work. Knit the next stitch, bringing the yarn to the back over the right-hand needle, as shown.

Between two purl stitches: Leave the yarn at the front of the work. Bring the yarn to the back over the right-hand needle and to the front again, as shown. Purl the next stitch.

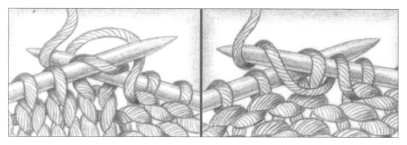

Multiple yarn overs (two or more): Wrap the yarn around the needle, as when working a single yarn over, then continue wrapping the yarn around the needle as many times as indicated. Work the next stitch of the left-hand needle. On the following row, work stitches into the extra yarn overs as described in the pattern. The illustration at right depicts a finished yarn over on the purl side.

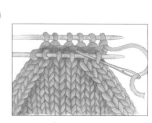

KITCHENER STITCH (GRAFTING)

1. Insert tapestry needle purlwise (as shown) through first stitch on front needle. Pull yarn through, leaving that stitch on knitting needle.

2. Insert tapestry needle knitwise (as shown) through first stitch on back needle. Pull yarn through, leaving stitch on knitting needle.

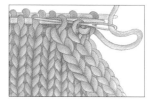

3. Insert tapestry needle knitwise through first stitch on front needle, slip stitch off needle and insert tapestry needle purlwise (as shown) through next stitch on front needle. Pull yarn through, leaving this stitch on needle.

4. Insert tapestry needle purlwise through first stitch on back needle. Slip stitch off needle and insert tapestry needle knitwise (as shown) through next stitch on back needle. Pull yarn through, leaving this stitch on needle.

Repeat steps 3 and 4 until all stitches on both front and back needles have been grafted. Fasten off and weave in end.

CHAIN STITCH (CROCHET)

1. Draw the yarn through the loop on the hook by catching it with the hook and pulling it toward you.

2. One chain stitch is complete. Lightly tug on the yarn to tighten the loop if it is very loose, or wiggle the hook to loosen the loop if it is tight. Repeat from step 1 to make as many chain stitches as required for your pattern.

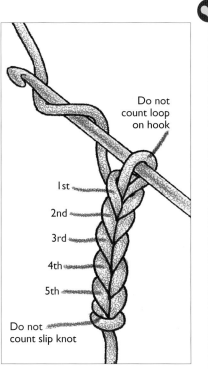

Do not count loop on hook

1st
2nd
3rd
4th
5th

Do not count slip knot

3. To count the number of chain stitches made, hold the chain so that the Vs are all lined up. Do not count the loop on the hook or the slip knot you made when beginning the chain. Each V counts as one chain made.

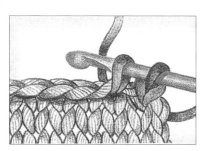

SINGLE CROCHET

1. Draw through a loop as for a slip stitch, bring the yarn over the hook, and pull it through the first loop. *Insert the hook into the next stitch and draw through a second loop.

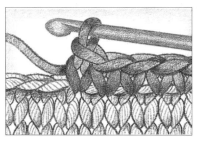

2. Yarn over and pull through both loops on the hook. Repeat from the * to the end.

▲ Ruffled Pullover (page 2)

I-CORD

Cast on about three to five sitches. *Knit one row. Without turning the work, slip the stitches back to the beginning of the row. Pull the yarn tightly from the end of the row. Repeat from the * as desired. Bind off.

TWISTED CORD

Cut two long strands of yarn at least three times the desired length of the cord. Attach them to something stationary and twist the free end many times until the yarn begins to kink up on itself. Fold the pieces in half and knot the ends together.

▲ One hank of yarn will allow you to make dozens of dresses—make one for all your loved ones!

Mini red dress

This tiny dress designed by Loretta Dachman is a knit version of *The Heart Truth*® logo. Wear it as a pin or hang it on the Christmas tree as a reminder of the importance of heart health!

MEASUREMENTS
BUST Approx 3"/7.5cm
LENGTH Approx 4½"/11.5cm

MATERIALS
• 1 3½oz/100g hank (each approx 1,531yd/1,400m) of Filatura Di Crosa *Centolavaggi* (superwash merino wool) in #125 ruby ⓪
• Small amount of white yarn
• One set (4) size 2 (2.75mm) double-pointed needles (dpns) *or size to obtain gauge*
• Stitch markers
• Stitch holder

GAUGE
36 sts and 56 rows to 4"/10cm over St st.
➤Take time to check gauge.

NOTE
You will need only about 30yd/27m of yarn to knit the dress.

DRESS
Cast on 40 sts. Divide sts over 3 needles as foll: 20 sts on needle 1, 10 sts each on needles 2 and 3. Join, taking care not to twist sts on needles, pm for beg of rnd.
Next rnd *K1, p1; rep from * around.
K 6 rnds.
Dec rnd [K2, k2tog, k12, k2tog, k2] twice—36 sts.
K 6 rnds.
Dec rnd [K2, k2tog, k10, k2tog, k2] twice—32 sts.
K 6 rnds.
Dec rnd [K2, k2tog, k8, k2tog, k2] twice—28 sts.
K 6 rnds.
Dec rnd [K2, k2tog, k6, k2tog, k2] twice—24 sts.
K 5 rnds.
Next rnd [K1, M1, k10, M1, k1] twice—28 sts.
K 1 rnd.
Next rnd [K1, M1, k12, M1, k1] twice—32 sts.
K 5 rnds.

DIVIDE FOR FRONT AND BACK
Note Work back and forth in rows over the 16 sts on needle 1.
K 1 row. p 1 row.
Next row K2tog, k3, join a 2nd ball of yarn and bind off 6 sts purlwise, k2, k2tog. Do not turn.

I-CORD STRAPS
(make 1 each side)
With dpns, work I-cord as foll:
*Next row (RS) With 2nd dpn, k4, do not turn. Slide sts back to beg of needle to work next row from RS; rep from * for 1"/2.5cm.
Cut yarn, leaving long tails for grafting, and place sts on holder.

BACK
Slip rem 16 sts on to one dpn. Join yarn.
K 1 row. p 1 row.
Next row K2tog, k3, bind off 6 sts purlwise, k2, k2tog. Graft live sts from I-cord with corresponding live sts on back.

FINISHING
Weave in ends. Block lightly. With white yarn, embroider a heart on left front.❤

To locate retailers, contact the manufacturers listed below.

ARTYARNS
39 Westmoreland Avenue
White Plains, NY 10606
www.artyarns.com

BERROCO, INC.
1 Tupperware Drive, Suite 4
North Smithfield, RI 02896-6815
www.berroco.com

BE SWEET
1315 Bridgeway
Sausalito, CA 94965
www.besweetproducts.com

BROOKLYN TWEED
www.brooklyntweed.net

CLASSIC ELITE YARNS
16 Esquire Road, Unit 2
North Billerica, MA 01862-2500
www.classiceliteyarns.com

COATS & CLARK
CONSUMER SERVICES
P. O. Box 12229
Greenville, SC 29612-0229
www.coatsandclark.com

U.K.: P. O. Box 22
Lingfield House
Lingfield Point, McMullen Road
Darlington County
Durham DL1 1YQ
England

CORNELIA HAMILTON
Distributed by Hamilton Design
Canada: Distributed by Diamond
Yarns

CRYSTAL PALACE YARNS
160 23rd Street
Richmond, CA 94804
www.crystalpalaceyarns.com

DEBBIE BLISS
www.debbieblissonline.com
Distributed by KFI

DEBORAH NORVILLE
COLLECTION
Distributed by Premier Yarns

DIAMOND YARNS
155 Martin Ross, Unit 3
Toronto, ON M3J 2L9
Canada
www.diamondyarn.com

FAIRMOUNT FIBERS, LTD.
P. O. Box 2082
Philadelphia, PA 19103
www.fairmountfibers.com

FILATURA DI CROSA
Distributed by Tahki•Stacy
Charles, Inc.

HAMILTON DESIGN
Storgatan 14
64730 Mariefred
Sweden
www.hamiltondesign.biz

JADE SAPPHIRE
EXOTIC FIBRES
www.jadesapphire.com

KFI
P. O. Box 336
315 Bayview Avenue
Amityville, NY 11701
www.knittingfever.com

KOIGU WOOL DESIGNS
P. O. Box 158
Chatsworth, OH N0H 1G0
Canada
www.koigu.com

LORNA'S LACES
4229 North Honore Street
Chicago, IL 60613
www.lornaslaces.net

MANOS DEL URUGUAY
www.manos.com.uy
Distributed by
Fairmount Fibers, Ltd.

MUENCH YARNS, INC.
1323 Scott Street
Petaluma, CA 94954-1135
www.myyarn.com

PLYMOUTH YARN CO.
500 Lafayette Street
Bristol, PA 19007
www.plymouthyarn.com

PREMIER YARNS
284 Ann Street
Concord, NC 28025
www.premieryarns.com

ROWAN
www.knitrowan.com
Distributed by
Westminster Fibers

U.K.: Green Lane Mill
Holmfirth, West Yorkshire
HD9 2DX
England

SHIBUI KNITS, LLC.
1500 NW 18th, Suite 110
Portland, OR 97209
www.shibuiknits.com

SMC SELECT
www.knitsmc.com
Distributed by
Westminster Fibers

STITCH NATION
BY DEBBIE STOLLER
Distributed by Coats & Clark

SWANS ISLAND YARNS
231 Atlantic Highway
(Route 1)
Northport, ME 04849
www.swansislandblankets.com

TAHKI YARNS
Distributed by Tahki•Stacy
Charles, Inc.

TAHKI•STACY CHARLES, INC.
70-30 80th Street, Building 36
Ridgewood, NY 11385
www.tahkistacycharles.com

TRENDSETTER YARNS
16745 Saticoy Street, Suite 101
Van Nuys, CA 91406
www.trendsetteryarns.com

Canada: Distributed by
The Old Mill Knitting Company
P. O. Box 81176
Ancaster, Ontario
Canada L9G 4X2
www.oldmillknitting.com

UNIVERSAL YARN
284 Ann Street
Concord, NC 28025
www.universalyarn.com

WESTMINSTER FIBERS
165 Ledge Street
Nashua, NH 03060
www.westminsterfibers.com

index

CREDITS

PORTRAITS OF DESIGNERS
p. 2: Courtesy of Rowan
p. 6: Bruce Cook
p. 8: Jonathan Law
p. 12: Peter Ralston
p. 15: Jose Arevelo
p. 19: Tiffany Hoffman
p. 22: Kiley Howard
p. 26: Tom Wool
p. 30: Gene Oakes
p. 32: Sandra Burkett
p. 36: Keith Brofsky
p. 39: Chris Vaccaro
p. 43: Richard Burns
p. 46: Selma Moss-Ward
p. 52: Roger Chang
p. 54: Rebecca Redston
p. 57: Timothy Sanders White
p. 60: Rose Callahan
p. 64: Maschenkunst
p. 68: Jared Flood
p. 72: Tiffany Hoffman
p. 74: Michael Luppino
p. 77: Courtesy of Rowan
p. 81: Carrie Bostick Hoge
p. 84: Courtesy of NBC Sports
p. 87: Elliot Schreier
p. 90: Aliya Naumoff
p. 93: Sandra Tiano
p. 96: Courtesy of Rowan
p. 98: Taiu Landra

SPECIAL THANKS TO
p. 27:
Hand-dyed wooden bead
necklaces by Ruth Feldman
rfeldman212@gmail.com

p. 97:
Ballet pointe shoes donated by
Gaynor Minden New York
www.gaynorminden.com
212-929-0087

♥ ACKNOWLEDGMENTS

I am forever grateful to many people for their help in putting this book together. I had heard that no book is ever the product of one person's efforts, and my experience with this book certainly confirmed that. *Knit Red* is the result of the efforts of nearly one hundred people: the designers, the yarn companies, the folks at Sixth&Spring Books, and, most important—my heroes—the girls at Jimmy Beans Wool.

At the top of my list of individuals to thank are three people, for without any one of them, this book would not have happened: Trisha Malcolm (Editorial Director of *Vogue® Knitting* and Publisher of Sixth&Spring Books), for responding with such passion and enthusiasm to the idea of *Knit Red*. Your reaction was so infectious that you made us believe we could do anything!

Debbie Bliss, for not only being the first designer to listen to the idea, but also the first to jump on board. Without your encouragement and feedback I might not have had the courage to ask anyone else.

Bethany Steiner (Jimmy Beans Wool), for being the perfect organizational complement to my messy brain, for putting your heart and soul into this book, and for taking the *Knit Red* concept and turning it into a book the whole industry can be proud of.

To all of the yarn companies represented in the book, thank you. I know that my crazy ideas can get tiresome at times, and I sincerely appreciate the never-ending (and seemingly unconditional) trust and support that I got from all of you during this process. Specifically, thanks to the folks at Artyarns, Berroco, Be Sweet, Brooklyn Tweed, Classic Elite Yarns, Cornelia Hamilton, Crystal Palace Yarns, Debbie Bliss, Deborah Norville Collection, Jade Sapphire Exotic Fibres, Koigu Wool Designs, Lorna's Laces, Manos del Uruguay, Muench Yarns, Plymouth Yarns, Red Heart/Coats & Clark, Rowan, Shibui, SMC Select, Swans Island, Tahki • Stacy Charles, Trendsetter, and Universal Yarn.

I'd also like to reiterate my thanks to those that I admire the most in this world: the girls and boys (and puppies!) I work with at Jimmy Beans Wool. Ralph Waldo Emerson once wrote, "Every man I meet is in some way my superior," and that has been my exact experience. Each day, I learn something new from all of you, and I am eternally honored to be a part of your lives.

And, finally, I'd like to thank the designers. *Knit Red* wouldn't have been possible without all your contributions. Thank you for believing in me, in Jimmy Beans Wool, and in the idea that when we all come together, we can change the world. The next glass of heart-healthy red wine is on me! ♥